Brigitte Steger and Angelika Koch (eds)

Manga Girl Seeks Herbivore Boy

D1565408

Japanologie / Japanese Studies

Band / Volume 3

LIT

Manga Girl
Seeks Herbivore Boy

Studying Japanese Gender
at Cambridge

edited by

Brigitte Steger and Angelika Koch

LIT

Cover design by Sven Palys, with manga by Denise Telalagic

Type-set by Barry Plows and Brigitte Steger

Printed with the financial support of the Japanese Studies Fund of the Faculty of Asian and Middle Eastern Studies, University of Cambridge; acknowledged with gratitude

Bibliographic information published by the Deutsche Nationalbibliothek
The Deutsche Nationalbibliothek lists this publication in the Deutsche Nationalbibliografie; detailed bibliographic data are available in the Internet at http://dnb.d-nb.de.

ISBN 978-3-643-90319-8

A catalogue record for this book is available from the British Library

©LIT VERLAG GmbH & Co. KG Wien,
Zweigniederlassung Zürich 2013
Klosbachstr. 107
CH-8032 Zürich
Tel. +41 (0) 44-251 75 05
Fax +41 (0) 44-251 75 06
E-Mail: zuerich@lit-verlag.ch
http://www.lit-verlag.ch

LIT VERLAG Dr. W. Hopf
Berlin 2013
Fresnostr. 2
D-48159 Münster
Tel. +49 (0) 2 51-62 03 20
Fax +49 (0) 2 51-23 19 72
E-Mail: lit@lit-verlag.de
http://www.lit-verlag.de

Distribution:
In Germany: LIT Verlag Fresnostr. 2, D-48159 Münster
Tel. +49 (0) 2 51-620 32 22, Fax +49 (0) 2 51-922 60 99, E-mail: vertrieb@lit-verlag.de
In Austria: Medienlogistik Pichler-ÖBZ, e-mail: mlo@medien-logistik.at
In Switzerland: B + M Buch- und Medienvertrieb, e-mail: order@buch-medien.ch
In the UK: Global Book Marketing, e-mail: mo@centralbooks.com
In North America: International Specialized Book Services, e-mail: orders@isbs.com

TABLE OF CONTENTS

TABLE OF CONTENTS

PREFACE AND ACKNOWLEDGEMENTS

Brigitte Steger

This volume is a new and exciting departure for Japanese Studies at the University of Cambridge: a collection of ground-breaking essays written by the latest crop of bright young scholars. Each is a recent graduate researching in gender-related areas: Hattie Jones and Zoya Street graduated in 2010, Nicola McDermott in 2011 and Chris Deacon in 2012.

All of the studies here explore fascinating aspects of Japanese society and culture that have either not been explored in this depth before or not at all. All are thoroughly researched, using a range of Japanese-language primary sources, contributing at a high level to the study of gender in Japan. They make fascinating reading, and are as accessible to those with little knowledge of Japan or Gender Studies as they are illuminating to those with a long-standing interest in these areas. Each of these essays originally formed the most significant part of the authors' undergraduate work – supervised by Mark Morris and myself – and each has refined and developed their work especially for this publication.

Beside the four authors, others have contributed to this book. I have co-edited this book with Angelika Koch, a PhD student in her final year working on sexuality and health discourse in pre-modern Japan. Rebekah Clements, a post-doctoral researcher in the department, has done the language-editing, and Katja Schmidtpott, a Temporary Lecturer in Modern History, helped with proof-reading. Sven Palys, himself a graduate of 2010, designed the cover, for which Denise Telalagic contributed the manga with her artistic skills and enthusiasm. Finally, I am indebted to the publishing expertise of Barry Plows for his inspiration on the title and technical advice on type-setting this book.

Brigitte Steger

About Japanese Studies at the University of Cambridge

At just 65 years old, the study of Japan at Cambridge is a relatively recent addition to the University compared with a long tradition of Arabic, Hebrew and Chinese Studies. In October 1947, the first two students embarked on the study of Japanese language and culture.[1] Both the lecturer, Eric Ceadel, and the students had switched from studying Latin and classical Greek; so it is perhaps no surprise that they thought that only the study of classical language and literature could be regarded as serious academic work.

Since then, Japanese Studies at Cambridge has become famous for the study of premodern literature and culture. With Richard Bowring (who has recently retired from the chair), Peter Kornicki and Laura Moretti (who has joined in 2012), the department continues to be world-leading in this area. Kornicki is now the Chair of Japanese Studies, and his main interest is in the history of the book and literacy, in how Chinese books have been read and ideas have spread all over premodern East Asia. Moretti specialises in commercial and popular prose of the seventeenth century, comprising didactic literature, graphic prose and ephemera. Currently two postdoctoral researchers complement their research on Tokugawa Japan: Rebekah Clements works on the cultural history of translation and Gerhard Leinss explores the use of calendars and almanacs.

However, with six tenured teaching positions and two full-time language teachers (Haruko Laurie and Toshimi Boulding), Cambridge provides a much wider range of research and teaching, including modern and contemporary Japan. Barak Kushner teaches modern history and is running a large research project on 'The Dissolution of the Japanese Empire and the Struggle for Legitimacy in Post-war East Asia, 1945–1965' (supported by the

---

[1] http://www.ames.cam.ac.uk/deas/japanese/fifty_years.pdf.
[2] 'Tentacle rape' is a type of pornography primarily found in Japan that depicts

4

European Research Council), while John Swenson-Wright is a specialist in Politics and International Relations of both Japan and Korea (North and South) whose insight is much in demand with the Chatham House political think-tank and the Foreign Office.

With this book we want to present a side of Japanese Studies at Cambridge that is perhaps little known: the study of Japanese society and culture, or more specifically, Gender Studies. Mark Morris is the Lecturer in East Asian Cultural History, whose interest and expertise in both literature and film has helped generations of students to sharpen their analytical skills and intellect in this area. I am teaching the courses on Japanese society and am mainly interested in questions of the cultural and social embeddness of seemingly natural matters and in daily life, investigating issues such as cleanliness, sleep and time-use.

We hope that this book helps to tell the story of what we are doing at Cambridge. We also hope that it inspires students and young scholars and is a supportive companion when they try their own first steps in academic research on Japan.

Cambridge, 12 December 2012

1. INTRODUCTION: GENDER MATTERS

Angelika Koch and Brigitte Steger

Samurai and Geisha. Madame Butterfly and the forty-seven *rōnin*. Uniformed school girls and *otaku* boys. The Japanese salaryman (*sarariiman*) in suit and neck-tie. Manga girls and herbivore boys. Many of the cultural images and stereotypes that have come to signify Japan in the West are deeply gendered concepts – some more overtly so, others less. Some of these images implicitly also conjure up connotations of a specific gender order – of obedient, exotic beauties of the past, of the pervasive post-war housewife and mother who manages the household of the toiling salaryman and the education of the children. Such simplistic views, however, cannot do justice to the complexity of gender identities in contemporary Japanese society, which have seen some changes and challenges in recent years. As Robin LeBlanc has argued, 'although none of the alternatives to "traditional" gender identities can be said to rival the [woman as] mother / [man as] breadwinner dichotomy for ascendancy, alternative ways of interpreting gender [...] now occupy increasing space in Japan' (LeBlanc 2011: 121).

Gender matters when talking or writing about Japanese society. If any quantitative proof were needed, one could for instance refer to the *Global Gender Gap Report 2012* released by the World Economic Forum, in which Japan ranks a hardly flattering 101st out of 135 countries surveyed – three positions down from last year, and by far the worst result of any of the G8 nations (World Economic Forum 2012). Statistically speaking, it would thus seem that living as a 'woman' or a 'man' in Japan still makes a big difference – at least in the four areas the report examined, that is economic participation, educational attainment, health and political empowerment.

Nevertheless, gender has not always been considered a significant issue in understanding Japanese society. There was a time 'before gender' when the universal male (heterosexual, elite) dominated as a subject of academic inquiry – in Japan just as much as in the West. Japanese *Nihonjinron* (theories of the Japanese) of the 1960s and 1970s, for instance, stressed the uniqueness and communalities of the Japanese regardless of age, class, gender, region or occupation (Befu 2001: 69), often creating projections of Japaneseness and Japan that were in actual fact profoundly gender-biased towards men (Morris-Suzuki 1998: 127).

Nakane Chie's classic study on *Japanese Society* (*Tate sha-kai no ningen kankei*; Nakane 1970) is an example par ex-cellence for the absence of gender. The society she outlines is essentially a society of men, or to be more precise, a society of white-collar, heterosexual salarymen – ironic maybe in view of the fact that the author herself is a woman who has infringed on a male-dominated domain, being the first female professor at the prestigious Tokyo University. Relegating women to minor remarks and footnotes, whilst dedicating a whole chapter to the 'characteristics and value orientation of Japanese man' (read as: salaryman), she constructs a society that effectively obliterates more than half of the population from the picture, given that Japanese women have persistently outnumbered men over the past decades. Moreover, no mention is made of those men and masculinities that for one reason or another did not quite fit this paradigmatic notion of the 'Japanese man'.

Four decades later, however, thinking about Japanese society – or any society, for that matter – without gender has become academically almost unviable, and more recent introductory ac-counts on the topic bear witness to this development (Robertson 2005; Sugimoto 2010; Bestor, Bestor and Yamagata 2011; Hendry 2012). During this period, the way we see gender has changed dramatically; it has come to be considered one of the central principles around which social life is organized, joining class and ethnicity as one of the master categories defining society. In this respect, gender can be seen as one counter-weight to earlier scholarship that, as Sugimoto puts it, 'attempted to generalize about Japanese society on the basis of observations of its male elite sector' (Sugimoto 2010: 2), a step away from what Befu has called the 'hegemony of homogeneity' (Befu 2001). The gender lens, in fact, has become a catalyst of plurality, which has directed its attention towards the diversity and differences that exist in society – between men and women, but increasingly also within the categories of men and women and beyond these categories across marginalized, queer gender identities. Significantly, concepts like genders, transgenders, masculinities, femininities and sexualities have in recent years often been used in the plural in scholarly discussions (Connell 2005; McLelland and Dasgupta 2005; Roberson and Suzuki 2003). In this way, they have therefore contributed to pushing discussions of social practices beyond a monolithic master narrative of hegemonic patterns.

Gender concerns gradually came into view in the social sciences in the wake of second-wave feminism, which in the 1970s began to posit 'gender' as the socially constructed domain opposed to the biological facts of 'sex'. Sex was the difference between male and female bodies in anatomy; gender the difference between feminine and masculine roles in social interaction – and the latter was not the natural outcome of the former. Thinking of the categories of men and women along these lines was a conceptual step forward, intended to cut the previous ties of an all-determining anatomy that 'dictated' a difference between the sexes. It was not the sex ascribed to the body that naturally encoded and produced a person's gender (Connell 2002: 30–36). Rather, it was society that construed what was 'masculine' and 'feminine', and therefore made men and women what they are – an approach that made gender and the processes that produced it a concern for the study of society.

Other theorists have seen the influence of culture as even more far-reaching; Judith Butler has famously argued in *Gender Trouble: Feminism and the Subversion of Identity* (1990) that it is not sex that determines gender, but rather gender that determines

9

what we call sex, suggesting that in the end 'perhaps this construct called "sex" is as socially constructed as gender' (Butler 1999 [1990]: 10). In this way, she effectively collapsed the distinction between sex and gender, the 'natural' and the 'cultural', that had informed the prevailing understanding of feminism in the 1970s and 1980s. Gender, to her, is produced 'performatively', through a 'stylized repetition of acts' (Butler 1999 [1990]: 179) that creates the illusion of a gender identity. In this view, gender thus becomes a doing, the miming of social norms of how men and women should behave – including notions of who they should desire as sexual objects. Gender performances that do not fit this normative heterosexual mould or 'matrix', such as drag, have subversive potential and expose the social constructedness of gender. They challenge the 'model of gender intelligibility', in which sex (male/ female) is seen to naturally give rise to the relevant (masculine/ feminine) gender identity, and to desire for the opposite sex (Butler 1999 [1990]: 23). In setting out to expose the problems of this presumed 'natural' coherence between sex, gender and desire, Butler thus also provided theoretical stimuli for queer theory, which emerged as a productive field of research from the early 1990s (see also chapters 4 and 5 in this volume).

How has gender left its mark on the field of Japanese Studies? In Japan, just as in the West, women and women's issues first emerged as a subject of scholarly work under the influence of the women's liberation movement, with the academic discipline of Women's Studies (*joseigaku*) developing from the 1970s onwards (Fujieda 1995; Mackie 2003: 162–164). Ever since then, a wealth of studies on Japanese women has been produced in Women's Studies and later in Gender Studies, which explore femininities in their historical dimensions (Bernstein 1991; Wakita, Bouchy and Ueno 1999; Tono-mura 1999; Molony 2005), as well as in their manifold modern and contemporary expressions (Ehara 1998, 2000; Inoue 1994–95). Classic studies like Ella Wiswell's *Women of Suye Mura* (Smith and Wiswell 1982) or Gail Lee Bernstein's *Haruko's World* (1983) began in the early 1980s to give a voice to the ordinary Japanese women hitherto unheard in research. Later work, drawing on the theoretical assumptions of Gender Studies, focused more on the relationships between women and men, as well as the processes and practices that brought forth gender in society. An exhaustive survey of the now well-stocked field would go beyond the scope of this introduction, but topics have included women and gender in the workplace (Kondo 1990; Ogasawara 1998), housewives and motherhood (LeBlanc 1999; Allison 1996, Imamura 1987; Goldstein-Gidoni 2012), Japanese women and internationalism (Kelsky 2001), women's – at times deviant – behaviour (Miller and Bardsley 2005; Bardsley and Miller 2011) and body practices (Miller 2006; Spielvogel 2003).

The lived realities of Japanese women (and men) are diverse and have begun to digress from post-war patterns of femininity, the family and the gendered division of labour. Nevertheless, there is still a wide-spread benchmark against which any recent reconfigurations need to be read, that is the overarching ideal of women as mothers nurturing the family (Uno 1993). During Japan's post-war economic growth, this role of women as managers of the middle-class household developed parallel to men's assignation as sole providers for the family. Women were in charge of children and domestic affairs; men dedicated their lives to work and company, whilst rarely spending any time at home, becoming absent partner and parent in a 'fatherless family' (Ishii-Kuntz 1992). In recent decades, however, the continuous drop in marriage as well as fertility rates, together with the rising divorce figures, demonstrate that this stereotypical life-style is increasingly on the retreat, representing what Karen Kelsky has called women's '"defection" from expected life courses' (Kelsky 2001: 2). Many women no longer consider marriage an integral part of their life, marrying later or in fact not at all – with statistics revealing that as of 2005 18.4 percent of Japanese females aged 35–39 had never been married (LeBlanc 2011: 120).

Beyond the exploration of these diverse female realities, previous research has also focused on representations of women in the media and popular culture, for instance in manga (Napier 1998; Allison 1996). Hattie Jones's contribution to this collection adds to this last strand of gender research, discussing the representations of women and gender roles in manga and anime aimed at young boys (*shōnen manga/anime*). Focusing on four different series, her analysis covers a spectrum of female images that the typical male consumer is confronted with in these media, which range from traditional, sexist takes on femininity, to more empowered visions of women. Jones' discussion overall reflects a saturation of the genre with gender norms that are conventional on many counts, as is evidenced in the types of images she isolates from her material. Thus she finds for instance pornographic images which commodify women's bodies for the sake of male erotic pleasure and bare them to the two-fold male gaze of the consumer and the fictional male characters. Women willingly subordinate themselves and are blatantly sexualised in these representations. Also common are fairy-tale structures that frame the male protagonists as heroic prince, and fix the woman in the complementary role of the powerless and clueless princess, who is to be ultimately subjugated to the man's will through the force of romance. Images of criminal women, on the other hand, are represented as in some way gender-deviant. Nevertheless, Jones also notes that humour in manga can serve to subvert traditional gender roles and reconfigure the gender order in making socially prescribed roles a target of fun.

Gender, however, is not always female – notwithstanding the fact that the term has often been used virtually as a synonym for 'women'. In fact, Japanese men and Japanese masculinities have become an increasingly flourishing field of academic interest in recent years, in English-speaking literature as well as in Japan itself (McLelland and Dasgupta 2005; Roberson and Suzuki 2003; Louie and Low 2003; Itō 1996; Taga 2006). Drawing on insights into the nature of gender from feminist scholarship, such research has moved past 'man' as merely the default category of academic analysis, whose manhood is uncritically taken for granted. Whilst this can be seen within a larger, international research trend towards making masculinity visible as a gendered, constructed ideology (Connell 2005; Kimmel 1996), Taga Futoshi has argued that the Japanese discipline of Men's Studies (*danseigaku*) was not merely the result of Western influences, but an indigenous development that arose in response to major social changes affecting Japanese men (Taga 2005).

Central among these was the economic downturn of the early 1990s, which dealt a heavy blow to 'traditional' post-war Japanese masculinity, understood as the white-collar corporate worker or salaryman (Hidaka 2010). As the economic prosperity of the 1980s bubble years gave way to recession, the hegemony of the life-style represented by the Japanese 'male employee in a suit', the human face of Japan's post-war economic boom, went into crisis. Rising unemployment rates, increasing numbers of work and redundancy related suicides amongst men, as well as media coverage on death by overwork (*karōshi*) began to undermine the desirability of the 'corporate warrior' identity, sparking the development of a 'men's liberation movement' in Japan and making space for alternative negotiations of masculinity (Taga 2005), although hegemonic notions still remain strong (Dasgupta 2005).

At the same time, Japan's chronically ailing birth rate also prompted the government to actively promote new facets of masculinity that went beyond the man as breadwinner and 'central supporting pillar' (*daikokubashira*) of his household. Based on the assumption that women might be more willing to engage in bearing and raising children when supported by their male partners, the government launched various campaigns in the late 1990s and 2000s, positing the 'nurturing father' as an ideal to supersede the stereotypical, hard-working 'absent father'. Nevertheless, whilst statistics suggest that an overwhelming majority of Japanese women as well as men now acknowledge participation of the father in child care as desirable, realities are slow to change (Ayami 2006), although some inroads have been made (Ishii-Kuntz 2003).

Zoya Street's thesis on moral education textbooks used in Japanese primary and middle schools charts a pocket of resistance to any such societal shifts in masculinities, ideological or real, as might have been underway in Japan in the past two decades. Her contribution to this collection demonstrates the persistence of traditional views on fatherhood in such textbooks, introducing us to representations of the typical post-war 'fatherless' family – which are in fact not quite as fatherless as one might expect. Analysing materials published over a thirty-year period between 1966 and 1996, she comes to the conclusion that the ideal father figure portrayed in these teaching materials remained largely unaltered, unswayed by competing new views on fatherhood in Japanese society. The father she finds in the short moral tales is the absent father – the traditional breadwinner for his family, who in his role as provider is rooted in the sphere outside the home. Despite his absence, however, the father is portrayed as a moral agent involved in the psychological growth of the child in the texts. Although he hardly talks, he understands the child very well; his judgement guiding it on its path to self-reliance and ethical action, as Street argues.

Christopher Deacon's contribution on 'herbivore boys' (*sō-shokukei danshi*), by contrast, traces a social phenomenon amongst young Japanese men that reflects the ongoing deconstruction of hegemonic masculinity and highlights a certain malaise felt amongst the younger generation of males vis-à-vis the orthodox 'salaryman doxa' (Roberson and Suzuki 2003), centred around corporate employment and marriage. Having gained currency as a media buzzword in the past five years, the term 'herbivore' re-presents an amalgamation of changes in the way some young Japanese men perform their gender – changes which have fre-quently led to criticism and moral panic that young men nowadays are not 'proper men' anymore. For not only do such tame 'grass-eaters' place little importance on relationships with women and therefore by implication also on marriage – still a hallowed precondition for becoming a full member of Japanese society (*shakaijin*) – they are often held to be uninterested in sex al-together, which is seen as a further cause for the population decline. Uncompetitive on the labour market, they find careers in the corporate world undesirable, thus also undermining the deep-rooted notion of work as the overarching meaning of a Japanese man's life. Outlining these current subversions of previously domi-nant masculine gender norms by such young men, who often actively reject the image of masculinity prevalent in their fathers' generation, Deacon's thesis captures a sense of the gender troubles stirred up by post-bubble men.

Lastly, Nicola McDermott's dissertation on transgenderism moves into the domain of genders that defy our common-sense understanding of the term as a binary of men and women – a domain, in Judith Butler's terms, outside the heterosexual matrix of 'intelligible' genders (Butler 1990). Marginalized genders and sexualities in Japan past and present have generally received lively attention, scholarly and otherwise, over the past two decades (Pflugfelder 1999; Leupp 1995; Welker 2004, 2008; Maree 2004; Mackintosh 2011; Chalmers 2002; Lunsing 2001; McLelland 2000, 2005, 2006; Kakefuda 1992). Starting with Fushimi Noriaki's publishing and media activities (Fushimi 1991), Japan itself wit-nessed a veritable 'gay boom' in the 1990s, which also swept across the mainstream media and made homosexuality more visi-ble, albeit often in a sensationalist fashion (McLelland 2000: 36–37). Yet as some scholars have critically noted, this increased attention mainly concerned gay men and was fundamentally characterized by an androcentric 'lesbian blindness' (Chalmers 2002: 31), contributing little to breaking the silence surrounding female same-sex desire. Transgenderism, on the other hand, has often been conflated with homosexuality in the media (McLelland 2000: 43), and scholarship on the topic in English and Japanese has only begun to appear over the past decade (McLelland 2003, 2004; Lunsing 2003, 2005; Mitsuhashi 2006, 2008; Ishida 2008).

McDermott adds to this newly emerging research on Japa-nese transgenderism, chronicling the situation of transgender peo-ple in post-war Japan, with a particular focus on two major legal and political changes that have affected transgender lives over the past two decades. This is, on the one hand, the resumption of sex reassignment surgery in 1998 after a thirty-year hiatus, and the legalisation of gender change on the household register (*koseki*) in 2003 on the other hand. Both decisions, although in principle desirable for Japanese transgender people, are deeply imbued with hetero-normative notions that show little understanding of transgender identities, as McDermott argues. Sex reassignment surgery requires a diagnosis of 'Gender Identity Disorder', which generally pathologizes transgender identities and presumes that the operation will fit individuals back into the binary moulds of 'male' and 'female', merely giving them the 'right' body for their gender performance. Legal gender change, on the other hand, has been restricted to unmarried and childless transgender individuals, seeking to protect the family as a hetero-normative domain. Both these changes perpetuate conservative views on gender and the family, and have caused criticism from transgender people, as McDermott shows.

Together, the essays gathered in this volume make a contribution to the study of various gender identities and their representations. They illustrate both the persistence of traditional ideals of what men and women should be like, as well as the rejection and resistance mounted to these hegemonic notions from various quarters in society. Read together, the individual snapshots of genders and sexualities that co-exist in contemporary Japanese society draw a picture of an ongoing negotiation of gender roles, a potential transformation in the making against the backdrop of continuing strong expectations of earlier values. The book paints a bigger picture that oscillates between the persistence of 'traditional' expectations and the challenges, reconfigurations, resistances and rejections facing them. Interestingly, whilst these challenges to received notions of gender and family are very real, sometimes the realm of representation can be a preserve of tradition lagging behind social shifts, as the small cross-section of research assembled in this volume would suggest. Other studies have noted a similar gap, albeit in different contexts; Takeda Hiroko has for instance recently argued that government discourses in Japan disregard life-styles outside the conventional notion of heterosexual marriage, glossing over the diversification observable in society (Takeda 2011). Social reality might thus be faster to change in some respects than idealized representations. Change, as this reminds us, is never a linear process, but can give rise to conflicting, diverse meanings that exist at the same time, reflecting the different attitudes and interests of various social groups. In this way, it becomes possible for figures like 'manga girls', 'herbivore boys', 'absent fathers' and transgender people to coexist in contemporary Japanese society.

References

Allison, Anne (1996). *Permitted and Prohibited Desires: Mothers, Comics and Censorship in Japan*. Boulder: Westview Press.

Bardsley, Jan and Laura Miller (2011 eds). *Manners and Mischief: Gender, Power and Etiquette in Japan*. Berkeley: University of California Press.

Befu Harumi (2001). *Hegemony of Homogeneity: An Anthropological Analysis of Nihonjinron*. Melbourne: TransPacific Press.

Bernstein, Gail Lee (1983). *Haruko's World: A Japanese Farm Woman and Her Community*. Stanford: Stanford University Press.

Bernstein, Gail Lee (1991 ed.). *Recreating Japanese Women, 1600–1945*. Berkeley: University of California Press.

Bestor, Victoria and Thedore Bestor, with Yamagata Akiko (2011 eds). *Routledge Handbook of Japanese Culture and Society*. London and New York: Routledge.

Butler, Judith (1999 [1990]). *Gender Trouble: Feminism and the Subversion of Identity*. London and New York: Routledge.

Chalmers, Sharon (2002). *Emerging Lesbian Voices from Japan*. London: RoutledgeCurzon.

Connell, R.W. (2002) *Gender*. Cambridge: Polity Press.

Connell, R.W. (2005). *Masculinities*. Berkeley: University of California Press.

Dasgupta, Romit (2005). 'Salarymen Doing Straight: Heterosexual Men and the Dynamics of Gender Conformity', Mark McLelland and Romit Dasgupta (eds) *Genders, Transgenders and Sexualities in Japan*. London and New York: Routledge, pp. 168–182.

Ehara Yumiko (1998). *Josei, bōryoku, nēshon* (Women, violence, nation). Tōkyō: Keisō Shobō.

Ehara Yumiko (2000). *Seishoku gijutsu to jendā* (Reproductive technology and gender). Tōkyō: Keisō Shobō.

Frühstück, Sabine and Anne Walthall (2011 eds). *Recreating Japanese Men*. Berkeley: University of California Press.

Fujieda Mioko and Kumiko Fujimura-Fanselow (1995). 'Women's Studies: An Overview', Kumiko Fujimura-Fanselow and Kameda Atsuko (eds) *Japanese Women: New Feminist Perspectives on the Past, Present and Future*. New York: Feminist Press at the City University of New York, pp. 155–180.

Fushimi Noriaki (1991). *Puraibēto gei raifu: Posuto renai-ron* (Private gay life. Post-love discourse). Tōkyō: Gakuyō Shobō.

Goldstein-Gidoni, Ofra (2012). *Housewives of Japan: An Ethnography of Real Lives and Consumerized Domesticity*. New York: Palgrave MacMillan.

Hendry, Joy (2012). *Understanding Japanese Society*. Fourth edition. London: Routledge.

Hidaka Tomoko (2010). *Salaryman Masculinity: The Continuity and Change in Hegemonic Masculinity in Japan*. Leiden: Brill.

Imamura, Anne (1987). *Urban Japanese Housewives: At Home and in the Community*. Honolulu: University of Hawaii Press.

Inoue Teruko, Ueno Chizuko and Ehara Yumiko (1994–1995 eds). *Nihon no feminizumu* (Japanese feminism). 8 vols. Tōkyō: Iwanami Shoten.

Ishida Hitoshi et al. (2008 ed.). *Seidō itsusei shōgai: Jendā, iryō, tokureihō* (Gender Identity Disorder: Gender, medical treatment and the *Special Act for the Treatment of the Gender of Individuals Suffering from Gender Identity Disorder*). Tōkyō: Ochanomizu Shobō.

Ishii-Kuntz, Masako (1992). 'Are Japanese Families "Fatherless"?', *Sociology and Social Research* 76/3, pp. 105–110.

Ishii-Kuntz, Masako (2003). 'Balancing Fatherhood and Work: Emergence of Diverse Masculinities in Contemporary Japan', James Roberson and Suzuki Nobue (eds) *Men and Masculinities in Contemporary Japan: Dislocating the Salaryman Doxa*. London, New York: RoutledgeCurzon, pp. 198–216.

Itō Kimio (1996). *Danseigaku nyūmon* (Introduction to Men's Studies). Tōkyō: Sakuhinsha.

Kakefuda Hiroko (1992). *Rezubian de aru to iu koto* (What it means to be lesbian). Tōkyō: Kawade Shobō Shinsha.

Kelsky, Karen (2001). *Women on the Verge: Japanese Women, Western Dreams*. Durham: Duke University Press.

Kimmel, Michael (1996). *Manhood in America: A Cultural History*. New York, London: Free Press.

Kondo, Dorinne K. (1990). *Crafting Selves: Power, Gender, and Discourses of Identity in a Japanese Workplace*. Chicago: University of Chicago Press.

LeBlanc, Robin (1999). *Bicycle Citizens: The Political World of the Japanese Housewife*. Berkeley: University of California Press.

LeBlanc, Robin (2011). 'The Politics of Gender in Japan', Victoria Lyon Bestor and Theodore Bestor, with Yamagata Akiko (eds) *Routledge Handbook of Japanese Culture and Society*. London and New York: Routledge, pp. 116–128.

Leupp, Gary (1995). *Male Colors: The Construction of Homosexuality in Tokugawa Japan*. Berkeley: University of California Press.

Louie, Kam and Morris Low (2003 eds). *Asian Masculinities: The Meaning and Practice of Manhood in China and Japan*. London: RoutledgeCurzon.

Lunsing, Wim (2001). *Beyond Common Sense: Sexuality and Gender in Contemporary Japan.* London: Kegan Paul International.

Lunsing, Wim (2003). 'What Masculinity? Transgender Practices Among Japanese Men', James Roberson and Suzuki Nobue (eds) *Men and Masculinities in Contemporary Japan. Dislocating the Salaryman Doxa.* London: RoutledgeCurzon, pp. 20–36.

Lunsing, Wim (2005). 'The Politics of *okama* and *onabe*: Uses and Abuses of Terminology Regarding Homosexuality and Transgender', Mark McLelland and Romit Dasgupta (eds) *Genders, Transgenders and Sexualities in Japan.* London: Routledge, pp. 81–95.

Mackie, Vera (2003). *Feminism in Modern Japan: Citizenship, Embodiment and Sexuality.* Cambridge: Cambridge University Press.

Mackintosh, Jonathan D. (2011). *Homosexuality and Manliness in Post-war Japan.* London: Routledge.

Maree, Claire (2004). 'Same-sex Partnerships in Japan. Bypasses and Other Alternatives', *Women's Studies* 33, pp. 541–549.

McLelland, Mark (2000). *Male Homosexuality in Modern Japan: Cultural Myths and Social Realities.* London: RoutledgeCurzon.

McLelland, Mark (2003). 'Living More "Like Oneself": Transgender Identities and Sexualities in Japan', *Journal of Bisexuality* 3/3–4, pp. 203–230.

McLelland, Mark (2004). 'From the Stage to the Clinic: Changing Transgender Identities in Post-war Japan', *Japan Forum* 16/1, pp. 1–20.

McLelland, Mark (2005). *Queer Japan from the Pacific War to the Internet Age.* Lanham: Rowman and Littlefield.

McLelland, Mark and Romit Dasgupta (2005 eds). *Genders, Transgenders and Sexualities in Japan.* London: Routledge.

McLelland, Mark (2006 ed.). *Intersections: Gender, History and Culture in the Asian Context* 12. Queer Japan Special Issue.

Miller, Laura (2006). *Beauty Up: Exploring Contemporary Japanese Body Aesthetics.* Berkeley: University of California Press.

Miller, Laura and Jan Bardsley (2005 eds). *Bad Girls of Japan.* New York: Palgrave Macmillan.

Mitsuhashi Junko (2006). 'The Transgender World in Contemporary Japan. The Male to Female Cross-dressers' Community in Shinjuku', *Inter-Asia Cultural Studies* 7/2, pp. 202–227.

Mitsuhashi Junko (2008). *Josō to Nihonjin* (Female cross-dressing and the Japanese). Tōkyō: Kōdansha.

Molony, Barbara and Kathleen Uno (2005 eds). *Gendering Modern Japanese History.* Cambridge, MA: Harvard University Asia Centre.

Morris-Suzuki, Tessa (1998). *Re-inventing Japan: Time, Space, Nation.* Armonk: M.E. Sharpe.

Nakatani, Ayami (2006). 'The Emergence of "Nurturing Fathers": Discourses and Practices of Fatherhood in Japan', Marcus Rebick and Takenaka Ayumi (eds) *The Changing Japanese Family.* London: Routledge, pp. 94–108.

Nakane Chie (1970). *Japanese Society.* Berkeley: University of California Press.

Napier, Susan (1998). 'Vampires, Psychic Girls, Flying Women and Sailor Scouts', D. P. Martinez (ed.) *The Worlds of Japanese Popular Culture: Gender, Shifting Boundaries and Global Culture.* Cambridge: Cambridge University Press, pp. 91–109.

Ogasawara Yuko (1998). *Office Ladies and Salaried Men: Power, Gender and Work in Japanese Companies.* Berkeley: University of California Press.

Pflugfelder, Gary (1999). *Cartographies of Desire: Male-male Sexuality in Japanese Discourse 1600–1950.* Berkeley: University of California Press.

Roberson, James and Suzuki Nobue (2003 eds). *Men and Masculinities in Contemporary Japan: Dislocating the Salaryman Doxa.* London: RoutledgeCurzon.

Robertson, Jennifer (2005 ed.). *A Companion to the Anthropology of Japan.* Malden: Blackwell.

Smith, Robert John and Ella Lury Wiswell (1982). *The Women of Suye Mura.* Chicago: University of Chicago Press.

Spielvogel, Laura (2003). *Working Out in Japan: Shaping the Female Body in Tokyo Fitness Clubs*. Durham: Duke University Press.

Sugimoto Yoshio (2010). *An Introduction to Japanese Society*. Third edition. Melbourne: Cambridge University Press.

Taga Futoshi (2005). 'Rethinking Japanese Masculinities: Recent Research Trends', Mark McLelland and Romit Dasgupta (eds) *Genders, Transgenders and Sexualities in Japan*. London: Routledge, pp. 153–167.

Taga Futoshi (2006). *Otokorashisa no shakaigaku. Yuragu otoko no raifukōsu* [Sociology of manliness. The unstable life course of men]. Kyōto: Sekai Shisō-sha.

Takeda Hiroko (2011). 'Reforming Families in Japan. Family Policy in the Era of Structural Reform', Richard Ronald and Allison Alexy (eds) *Home and Family in Japan. Continuity and Transformation*. London: Routledge, pp. 46–64.

Tonomura Hitomi, Anne Walthall and Wakita Haruko (1999 eds). *Women and Class in Japanese History*. Ann Arbor: Centre of Japanese Studies, the University of Michigan.

Uno, Kathleen S. (1993). 'Death of "Good Wife, Wise Mother"?', Andrew Gordon (ed.) *Post-war Japan as History*. Berkeley: University of California Press, pp. 293–322.

Wakita Haruko, Anne Bouchy and Ueno Chizuko (1999 eds). *Gender and Japanese History*. Osaka: Osaka University Press.

Welker, James (2004). 'Telling Her Story. Narrating a Japanese Lesbian Community', *Japanstudien* 16, pp. 119–144.

Welker, James (2008). 'Lilies of the Margin. Beautiful Boys and Queer Female Identities in Japan', Fran Martin et al. (eds) *AsiapacifiQueer. Rethinking Genders and Sexualities*. Chicago: University of Illinois Press, pp. 46–66.

World Economic Forum (2012). *Global Gender Gap Report 2012*. http://www3.weforum.org/docs/WEF_GenderGap_Report_2 012.pdf

2 Manga Girls

Sex, Love, Comedy and Crime in Recent Boys' Anime and Manga

Hattie Jones

Supervisor: Mark Morris (2010)

Table of Contents

INTRODUCTION: BOYS' MANGA AS A RESOURCE FOR GENDER STUDIES

'Boys' manga', or *shōnen manga*, are aimed primarily at boys in their early to late teens. At this age, they will typically undergo puberty and develop an interest in girls. Much of this interest is supposedly concerned with how they can relate to girls in romantic and sexual situations. Thus, their exposure to male-female relations in the mass media as well as in everyday life will inform and shape their perceptions of women and how to approach them. Boys' manga, often starring teenage male protagonists, frequently address the idea of burgeoning male-female relationships. However most boys' manga are related from the perspective of the male, and researchers such as Anne Allison (1996) and Susan Napier (1998) have criticised the depiction of women and the presentation of the interaction between the sexes as sexist, out-dated and representing negative stereotypes, whether consciously or not. Their criticisms were levelled at boys' manga of the 1980s and 1990s. In this essay I seek to establish whether early twenty-first century boys' manga have changed in this respect and whether they depict women in a more varied, positive and realistic way.

The development of such a change in the depiction of women and the precise reasons why such a change might be occurring are beyond the scope of this essay to explore in detail. However they can be supposed to include both social and economic reasons. Social reasons include modernisation and liberalisation of public conceptions of women, brought about by the 'trickle-down' effect of laws such as the Equal Employment Opportunity Act of 1986/1999, feminist movements and the increased role of women in professional and political spheres (see for example Bishop 2005: 198–200). Economic reasons include the popularity of many nominally male-oriented manga series with female consumers and the desire of authors and publicists to engage with and benefit from this new and growing audience. Another important trend has been the diversification of available (and acceptable) masculinities, which has allowed men to construct and relate to new masculine identities that were once unrepresented or unendorsed by the mass media (see Deacon in the volume).

In assessing whether the representations of women in anime and manga have progressed beyond one-dimensional, idealised and sexualised depictions, I shall first discuss previous works assessing the presentation of gender in anime and manga. I shall then analyse the encoding of female characters by male authors in the context of four narratives in four popular boys' anime and manga series.

The Japanese comic art form 'manga' (and its animated equivalent 'anime') have been recognised increasingly in recent years as a valuable field for sociological and literary research. According to government statistics, manga comprised 36.7 percent of all material published in 2007 (Zenkoku Shuppan Kyōkai & Shuppan Kagaku Kenkyūjo 2007), but its aesthetics and influences are visible in all of Japan's contemporary cultural forms. Since 'audiences are generally oriented towards protecting and enlarging representations that resonate with them' (Harris 1998: 41), manga's enduring popularity within Japan would seem to indicate that it resonates with many people there. Certainly the animated form has achieved a popularity and legitimacy in Japan not found in the rest of the world (Toku 2007: 19). As an accessible, less 'realistic' art-form manga can, through fantasy and metaphor, (re)present the collective consciousness of Japanese society. As such, Frederik Schodt argues that '[r]eading manga is like peering into the unvarnished, unretouched reality of the Japanese mind' (Schodt 1996: 31).

The rise of feminist studies over the last few decades has led to much research on manga written by and aimed at girls (for example Napier 2001; Minako 2001). In contrast the study of boys' or *shōnen* manga (i.e. manga aimed at, and for the most part written by males) has generally been limited to pornography, salaryman stories and science fiction hits such as *Akira* and *Neon Genesis Evangelion* (see for example Allison 1996; Napier 2001). This essay will therefore address other, less well studied genres of boys' manga. There is perhaps an assumption that the study of women as written by men is 'anti-feminist', and that the women portrayed in boys' manga are not 'authentically female'. This may be true, but men's portrayal of women has value in and of itself as a subject for study, for 'the surface has its own truth' (Takahashi and Tsushima 2006: 120). Through its depictions of women and heterosexual relationships, boys' manga provides an insight into male perceptions of Japan's changing gender dynamic.

It is impossible to conduct any in-depth study that is truly representative of a genre the size of boys' manga. By choosing works that are 'popular', however, one can suppose some degree of cultural relevance. 'Popularity' is difficult to measure empirically, but of the four works I will discuss below, three originated in Japan's best-selling manga magazine *Shūkan Shōnen Janpu* (Boys' Weekly Jump), which in 2008 had a circulation of 2.79 million (Zenkoku Shuppan Kyōkai & Shuppan Kagaku Kenkyūjo 2008). The other, *The Melancholy of Haruhi Suzumiya*, is a hit anime series, placing fourth on a 2006 poll of the Japanese public's favourite anime conducted by TV Asahi (Anime News Network 2006). All four series started serialisation within the past decade, were created and written by male authors and feature female characters prominently. I discuss the encoding of 'femininity' on female manga characters in *To Love-ru* and *The Melancholy of Haruhi Suzumiya* from two different but interlinked perspectives. First, I focus on the gendered meanings invested in the female body in the context of (pseudo-)pornographic narratives. Second, I explore the positioning of the female and the male within 'romance' as structured in a 'fairytale' narrative. I shall then look at the relationship between women and crime in the criminological narrative offered by *Demon Detective Neuro Nōgami*, where the female is represented as both criminal and crime-fighter. Finally I shall focus on gender incongruity in the humorous narrative of *Gintama*, exploring how 'the female' interfaces with 'the joke'. By doing this, I should be in a position to draw a conclusion as to whether recent depictions of women in boys' manga and anime are more varied than is perhaps assumed, given previous scholarly work. My findings will also provide an insight into the current attitudes towards gender within Japanese society by analyzing what depictions of women apparently resonate with the popular consciousness.

TO LOVE-RU AND THE MELANCHOLY OF HARUHI SUZUMIYA

To Love-ru is a manga series written by Saki Hasemi and illustrated by Kentarō Yabuki. It ran in *Shūkan Shōnen Janpu* from 2006 until 2009. The title is a play on the Japanese pronunciation of the English word 'trouble' as '*toraburu*', referencing the 'trouble' that the primary romantic interest Lala causes the male protagonist, whilst using the English verb 'to love' to clearly mark it as a 'romantic' series. The series was adapted into a 26-episode television anime which aired in 2008. I shall be using the more widely available anime remake as my reference.

To Love-ru is billed as a 'harem-style romantic comedy'. The 'comedy' is largely slapstick, the 'romance' more about repeated nudity than any deeper romantic turmoil, and the 'harem' format means that a single male protagonist is surrounded by a large number of beautiful girls. In *To Love-ru* the protagonist is an ordinary Japanese boy called Rito, whose everyday life is turned upside down by the sudden materialisation of a nude girl in his bathroom. She introduces herself as an alien princess called Lala, and declares that she wants to marry Rito (initially in order to stay on Earth, but she soon falls in love with him). Rito then has to deal with suitors coming to win Lala's heart and his own confused romantic feelings towards her, while coping with the attentions of various other female acquaintances.

The Melancholy of Haruhi Suzumiya (*Suzumiya Haruhi no Yūutsu*) was originally a series of light novels. The first was published in 2003, and it is still in serialisation. The series gained international popularity, however, through the anime adaptation, which I shall be using as my source of reference. Tokyo MX aired the fourteen episode long 'first season' of the anime in 2006; these episodes were later rebroadcast in a different order with fourteen new 'second season' episodes intermixed in 2009. Episode numbers, where given, refer to the original order of broadcasting on Japanese television.

I have classified *The Melancholy of Haruhi Suzumiya* as a 'romantic comedy' given its frequent use of humour and the romantic tensions that exist between several of the main characters. It is however unusual for this genre in that it contains strong science-fiction themes. The titular Suzumiya Haruhi is a high-school student uninterested in normal humans, who forms her own club, the SOS Brigade, in order to uncover supernatural beings. The events that follow are related by her male classmate Kyon who, having been forced by Haruhi to participate in the SOS Brigade, learns that its other members comprise a psychic, a time traveller and an alien. All have been sent by different universal agencies to monitor Haruhi while keeping their true identities hidden from her, for unbeknownst to herself, Haruhi possesses the power to create, alter and even end worlds. The SOS Brigade are thus charged with the task of providing her with enough mental stimulation in the current reality that she will not unwittingly wish it out of existence.

Gender and the Pornographic Narrative

Neither series is 18-rated or features explicit or implicit sexual intercourse. However *To Love-ru* in particular contains a strong 'pornographic narrative' as it

> takes the signs of pornographic discourse [...] and inte-grates them into the context of non-pornographic story structures. In this way, the sign of pornography (never explicitly delivered) comes to stand in for an entire pornographic subtext, a series of blanks which readers remain free to fill in for themselves. (Reynolds 1992: 34)

To Love-ru features censored nudity, sexual harassment and even hints of the infamous 'tentacle rape',[2] all tropes of Japanese hard-core pornography, but here packaged within the context of a non-pornographic story. *The Melancholy of Haruhi Suzumiya*, while containing fewer pornographic motifs, nevertheless draws upon some sexualised imagery in a way that is common in much anime and manga (as discussed in Allison 1996).

The Watcher and the Watched

Both series are related from the perspective of a male protagonist (Rito, in *To Love-ru*, and Kyon, in *The Melancholy of Haruhi Suzumiya*), but star a female character after whom the series is named: Lala is the primary 'love' interest and 'trouble' referenced in the pun *'To Love-ru'*, and Haruhi's name features in the title of each novel and all subsequent spin-offs. The female characters are thus central and the male characters peripheral, relegated to the role of 'watcher' while the female takes the role of 'actor' who is being watched.

'Watcher' is an ambiguous position, being passive in its relation to the actor who provides the stimulus for the drama, yet simultaneously active in that watching can be sexual, voyeuristic and ultimately intrusive, making the one who is watched into the 'object' of the act of watching. Anthropologist Anne Allison describes the watcher/watched relationship depicted in (male-oriented) anime in terms of three elements: gender (men look, women are looked at), power (looking is empowering, being looked at is disempowering) and sexuality (looking produces one's own sexual pleasure, being looked at produces another's sexual pleasure) (Allison 1996: 31). By showing male characters staring at the exposed bodies of female characters, anime transmits 'a formulation of sexuality that, as recreative, is for males but not

---

[2] 'Tentacle rape' is a type of pornography primarily found in Japan that depicts tentacled creatures engaging in sexual intercourse with (usually) female characters.

females, is inscribed on female bodies but not male bodies, and inscribes males but not females in positions of voyeur and consumer' (Allison 1996: 48). This 'formulation of sexuality' is repeatedly transmitted by *To Love-ru*'s copious female nudity, and can even be detected in *The Melancholy of Haruhi Suzumiya*, as Kyon is shown staring at fellow SOS Brigade member Asahina's body. In particular, the breasts and panties of female characters are depicted as the focus of male looking, explicitly sexualising the gaze (Allison 1996: 44). The female characters do not stare at the male characters' bodies, because females are not given the power or agency to be a (sexual) consumer or voyeur; for the male characters, however, their overt viewing of women is unchallenged and even implicitly encouraged through its frequent depiction. The motif of the male gazing upon the naked or sexualised body of the female is not unique to the two series studied here, but is common even in manga and anime ostensibly aimed at children in Japan (Allison 1996: 29) and certainly in those aimed at adolescent or young adult males.

While manga males may gaze frequently and with relative impunity upon the bodies of their female classmates, however, they are rarely if ever allowed to touch them. Male power is thus not an absolute in these series; it is constrained by ideas of social decorum imported from the realities of Japanese society, even though they may be somewhat warped in the manga world. This tension between the potential sexual power conveyed in the male gaze and their feelings of constraint when it comes to the exercise of this power is not new. Japanologist Alisa Freedman comments on Tayama Katai's 1907 novel *The Girl Fetish* which depicts that very tension: the male protagonist fantasises about having a relationship with one of the female students he gazes at on the train, but 'he is frustrated by social, psychological, and class constraints, and instead he tries to satisfy his desires by just looking' (Freedman 2002: 25). Social awkwardness towards the physical aspects of sex and voyeurism are hardly unique to Japan – the art critic John Berger, commenting on Western art noted that 'Men look at women. Women watch themselves being looked at' (quoted in Allison 1996: 35). However, Allison argues persuasively for there being close correlates between the toleration and encouragement of voyeurism in modern Japanese media and broader attitudes in Japanese society. She describes the increase in voyeuristic imagery as accompanying a de-emphasis on depictions of actual genital copulation and orgasm (even in pornographic manga), which structures a form of real-world male sexuality that does not interfere as much with the time of performance of a student or worker as would other formulations of sexuality (Allison 1996: 32). This is particularly pronounced in Japan because (for adult men) long work days 'allow workers no other time or space for sex than as a commodity' (Ōshima Nagisa, quoted in Allison 1996: 45).

Adolescent males, the primary target of anime and manga such as *To Love-ru* and other *Shūkan Shōnen Janpu* titles, face a similar situation as regards the school day and their study commitments. Both *To Love-ru* and *The Melancholy of Haruhi Suzumiya* depict in the positioning of their male characters the contradiction between the anime male's sexual desire and his simultaneous feeling of sexual constraint. Kyon does not get to touch Asahina, the object of his lust, although he frequently is shown gazing at her (concealed) breasts, and Rito freezes in shock, sweats and goes red every time he is confronted by a nude female classmate. His only physical contact with naked women is unintentional – he frequently touches their breasts unintentionally, but leaps away in shock when he realises what he has done. It is not a lack of sexual desire on their part, but low confidence and a sense of constraint by social mores that inform their inaction when confronted by the object of their desires. This arguably mitigates the power imbalance constructed between men and women in the watcher/watched relationship, since the male's power is always potential, rarely actualised.

It is not just the male characters in anime who watch the female, however, but the consumer who watches them watching her, or watches her through the males' eyes. Certainly in the case of

33

To Love-ru, it is likely that the majority of viewers are male. The consumption of anime thus constitutes an act of voyeurism in and of itself, and the female is doubly made the object of the 'male gaze'.

The Female Body

As a visual medium, anime transmits gendered messages through its use of images. The frequency with which the (semi-)nude female body is shown, in what circumstances it is shown, and what cinematographic techniques are used to portray it contribute to *To Love-ru*'s pornographic narrative. The opening credit sequence, played at the start of every episode, shows still shots of the female characters' crotches, breasts, and legs. Scenes of Lala's 'transformation' are a more sexually overt versions of those found in 'magical girl' works such as *Sailor Moon*, with Lala portrayed moaning as ropes squeeze her flesh in a shot reminiscent of bondage.

In catering to a consumer audience which is assumed to be almost entirely comprised of young to middle-aged males, women as 'other' are presented in a way that plays to male desires. She is reduced from 'woman' to 'the female body', this 'reduction to body' constituting a form of objectification (Langton 2009: 226), as one denies the female an existence not defined by her physicality. The use of close-up shots fragment her body from a single entity into a patchwork of sexually-encoded parts, each of which constitutes an object to stimulate the male consumer's desire. Ueno Chizuko explains this sexual codification of women's bodies by reference to an essay entitled 'Why do I desire miniskirts?' where the heterosexual male author's desire was stimulated even by men in miniskirts: since the miniskirt itself was 'coded' female, it acted as a trigger for his (hetero)sexual desire (Ueno and Nobuta 2004: 123). *To Love-ru* thus avoids blatant pornography while still objectifying the female characters in the same way as pornography by featuring close-ups of the female characters' breasts and crotches. Women are defined by their bodies, and their bodies are reduced to the level of 'things (fetishes) which produce male arousal' (Miya 1994: 240). This objectification is logically accompanied by commodification, as 'in a capitalist society every object in the world is assigned a value' (Ueno 1994: 20). This widens the power imbalance between the sexes further, as 'the gap between those people who contain the [sexual] stimulus (women) and those people who are stimulated by it (men), resembles the relationship between 'things' and 'people' (Amano 1984: 141), with women's bodies deciding their worth as sexual 'commodities' in relation to male 'consumers'.

This consumer/commodity relationship is explicitly referenced in *To Love-ru*. Rito inadvertently 'proposes' to Lala in the first episode by grabbing her breasts, which on her home planet apparently counts both as a wedding proposal and, if done again, its annulment. Presumably this means only men can propose and annul marriage, and do so by the sexual harassment of women. Lala's guardian Zastin then explains to Rito that there is a 'cooling off period' during which he can annul the engagement: 'Like when you buy something by mail-order and a different product from the one you expected is delivered, you can return the goods'. The gender relationship in marriage depicted by *To Love-ru* is thus explicitly compared to that of (female) object and (male) consumer, where the female is powerless to act or to deny the male's act. In addition, the ease with which males can negotiate marriage, and the conspicuous abundance of potential female marriage partners in *To Love-ru* soothes male fears regarding the increasing number of real-life Japanese women who eschew marriage in favour of pursuing a career (see Liddle and Nakajima 2000).

As 'the appearance demanded of women is [...] the "codification of sex"' (Ueno and Nobuta 2004: 151), the female body is socially pressured to conform to generalised notions of what constitutes (sexual) attractiveness. In a patriarchal society, these notions are established by men. Ueno Chizuko gives the example of the male-judged 'Miss' contests: 'The Miss contestants are not the possessors of "beauty". They were given "beauty" by the gaze of patriarchal men' (Ueno 1994: 21). Beauty is 'a standard created by male hands' which has become 'not a privilege but something compulsory' for success and happiness. This has 'alienated women towards beauty' (*bi e no sogai*), as society has deemed it the only way a woman can have value (Ueno 1994: 21). None of the women in *To Love-ru* questions the male-defined standard of beauty expected of them (which usually means slimness, large breasts, a youthful face and a willingness to show one's body without argument). In *To Love-ru*'s fifth episode the female characters even compete in a 'Miss'-style contest of looks judged by the male students. In *The Melancholy of Haruhi Suzumiya*, however, there is some parody of the conventional anime model of female beauty: Haruhi explicitly states that she recruited her class-mate Asahina for the SOS Brigade because Asahina embodies the traits prized in an (anime) female; childish appearance, wide-eyed expression and high-pitched, breathy, pre-teen voice, unrealistically large breasts. That these (often unrealistic) traits are embodied by all the sexually desirable women in *To Love-ru* and other male-oriented anime suggests that this is considered sexually attractive by Japanese (male) society. For men 'the "ideal" woman's body is no longer "real" – it is imaged on a computer' (Eisenstein 1998: 86), and this image is transmitted through the media, shaping women's perceptions of their own beauty. Pressured by society to embody these unrealistic concepts of beauty, for women '[w]ith no end to imaged perfection, there is likewise no end to the oppressiveness of perfection' (Eisenstein 1998: 86).

Female Sexuality and Passivity

In Japanese society there is still a 'strong idea that sex is something "done" to women by men' (McLelland 2000: 73). In *To Love-ru* the female characters frequently have their bodies exposed to or by the male characters, mostly unwillingly. Lala often strips voluntarily, but seems ignorant as to the meaning of her own nudity, expressing no explicit sexual desire of her own. The ideal is a woman whose body is sexually mature but whose mind is not, whose sexuality is 'still one of response to the active sexuality of a man' (Coward 1987, cited in Clammer 1995: 212). The reasons for this are perhaps located in men's own insecurities; Kenneth G. Henshall explains that in Japanese culture the two most frequent depictions of woman are 'the mother' and 'the virgin', both of whom will forgive the man and not criticise (sexual) inadequacy (Henshall 1999: 37). In *To Love-ru* it is in episode 24 when Lala is afflicted by a personality-warping illness that renders her so shy she cannot interact socially, and takes to hiding behind Rito like a child, that all her male classmates call her 'feminine' (*onnanoko-rashii*) and 'cute' (*kawaii*). Similarly Kyon's primary romantic interest is not the free-spirited and strong-willed Haruhi but docile, agreeable Asahina; happy to serve the other SOS Brigade members tea in her role as their 'flower of the workplace' (*shokuba no hana*) she admits that she does not understand her own job as a time agent but just does what her superiors tell her. Thus while characters such as Haruhi may exhibit a refreshing new type of active, boisterous and independent female personality, the subtext is that men will still prefer girls who embody (in an often exaggerated manner) socially normative concepts of 'femininity'.

The ideal woman should not only be sexually submissive, but submissive in other spheres also. Therefore in anime which contain a pornographic narrative, there is often strong invocation of women's role in the home as wives, mothers and domestics. While it is certainly true that wives and mothers are not necessarily submissive, in anime they are represented in this way, which reassures male viewers by ensuring that no challenge to male authority will be depicted. Indeed the depiction of domestic females in anime lends credence to the claims of feminists such as Germaine Greer and Betty Friedan that the role of housewife is 'the epitome of female non-identity and passivity' (Friedan, quoted in Genz 2009: 51). The gadgets Lala creates are mostly upgraded domestic appliances such as hoovers and freezers, and when Rito tells her in the fourth episode that he won't marry any girl who cannot cook, she greets him the next day and cooks for him in order to please him. In this scene Lala is actually naked beneath her apron (see Fig.1), a familiar symbol of domesticity. This reveals the ready conflation of the pornographic and domestic narratives in male-oriented anime, for 'sex and housework are similar as things demanded of women as services' by men (Amano 1984: 154).

Fig. 1: In *To Love-ru*, a barely-dressed Lala prepares to cook for a shocked Rito. Lala's breasts are disproportionately large, and her face conveys innocent surprise at Rito's reaction. Rito's positioning in the scene also channels the 'male gaze' – the viewer sees Lala from his view-point (Tokyo Broadcasting System 2008).

Confining women to the domestic sphere is perhaps intended to assuage male insecurities as woman become increasingly competitive and uncontrollable in the workplace and other social spheres. Domestic chores such as cooking invoke the traditional gendered division of labour; 'the trope of cooking is an important one [...] even in a frighteningly changeable world, women cooking suggests a fundamentally stable social order' (Napier 2001: 155). Anime such as *To Love-ru* thus reflect male idealism, with women bound to the domestic sphere, supporting rather than challenging male supremacy.

Rewriting the Male

In contrast to the more active and confident Lala and Haruhi, Rito and Kyon are emphatically 'normal'. In recent years these 'ordinary boy' protagonists have become the standard in male-oriented romance anime and they offer a scenario in which boys do not have to be especially intelligent, handsome or brave in order to 'get the girl'. That men do not have to be depicted as flawless prince-like figures in order to accomplish works of merit or be considered viable romantic partners is certainly a step in freeing men from the structures of traditional masculinity and in reassessing what is desirable in a man, as well as reassuring 'normal' male consumers that they, too, may succeed and find love. It has also given female characters more power to determine the status of their (romantic) relationships with men. The modern male protagonist's lack of romantic confidence is paralleled by a rising confidence on the part of women to accept and reject their advances, although it is still the male who is expected to take the active lead in a romantic relationship.

   Also, although some Japanese feminists claim that 'if one asks who guarantees that a man is a man, the answer is not woman but the homosocial conglomerate of men' (Ueno 2006: 432), in *To Love-ru* it is the female characters whom the male Ren consults in episode seven to establish what constitutes 'masculinity' (*otoko-*

39

rashisa). One of them answers that she does not know whether it is really 'manly', but 'someone who is kind to everyone' (*minna ni yasashiku dekiru hito ka na*), which is interesting since 'kindness' is usually described as a 'feminine' rather than a 'masculine' trait due to women's biological potential for motherhood and its association with childcare and nurture (Tokuhiro 2009: 77). Another girl suggests wearing *fundoshi* (the traditional Japanese undergarment) and another declares that manliness is all about muscles, answers which tie more closely into familiar constructions of masculine gender roles. For the most part however this progressive (and permissive) depiction of gender is only applied to the male characters, while the female characters of *To Love-ru* are still expected to be beautiful, domesticated and (sexually) passive.

Pornography and romantic fairytales are two different genres, which nevertheless share many similar features. Primarily, both nominally concern 'love', be it the 'love-making' of pornography or the 'true love' of fairytale. The pseudo-pornography of anime series such as *To Love-ru* is often deeply intertwined with 'purer' ideas of romantic love, and draws on images and conventions associated with fairytale romance. The two genres also share a communality of gender presentation in that both primarily depict women as passive, submissive, and (romantically and sexually) available to the man who approaches her.

Gender and the Fairytale Narrative

To Love-ru and *The Melancholy of Haruhi Suzumiya* are just two of many romantic anime (both male and female-oriented) which incorporate conventions of Western romantic fairytales, such as the 'knight in shining armour', the princess who waits patiently to be rescued by her prince, the idea of true love and the power of a kiss to save the princess's life. These fairytale narratives are invoked (both explicitly and implicitly) because they are perceived by mainstream society as the ultimate romantic narratives, a perception encouraged by the worldwide popularity of the Disney movies. That these fairytales in fact present a deeply reactionary formulation of male-female gender relationships is mainly overlooked. Susan Napier suggests that the enduring popularity of the fairytale narrative (from a male perspective) is due to the fact that '[i]n a world where women seem increasingly out of control, the notion that certain truths about love and relationships in which the male identity remains stable and the male ego is restored rather than destroyed may have more appeal than ever' (Napier 2001: 147). In fairytales, unlike real life, the destabilising influence these superficially powerful women exert on the conventional order is ultimately contained by the 'emotional subordination' of the female characters to the male (Napier 2001: 147). *To Love-ru* and *The Melancholy of Haruhi Suzumiya* both follow a fairytale plot structure: the female protagonist drives the action forward for most of the story but is inevitably relegated to the passive role before its close, with the prince's sudden appearance (or the sudden transformation of the normal boy into a prince) reinstating a socially normative male-female power dynamic. In this way, the invocation of the fairytale narrative lends the series a superficially 'romantic' aura, as it reverberates with existing media texts and conventional notions of what constitutes 'romance', but essentially serves to contain the power of the female characters and to prevent any radical exploration of gender.

The Prince and the Princess

Japanese feminist Wakakuwa Midori claims that, despite 'princess stories' (for example Western fairytales such as *Snow White* or *Sleeping Beauty*) being nominally focused on the princess herself, 'the protagonist of princess stories is the prince' (Wakakuwa 2003: 161). The princes in these stories are 'the kind of indiscreetly superficial guy who falls in love with the princess on the spot just because she is beautiful and proposes marriage immediately' (Saitō

2001: 147). The princess is denied an active role; since 'the prince is "that which loves", and because she is "that which is loved", from the start there is nothing she can do by herself' (Wakakuwa 2003: 46). In fairytales the passive 'waiting' (often in the form of sleep) of the female for the prince's love, his proposal of marriage, and ultimately his rescue, places by default the male as the protagonist of any romantic narrative. Despite being nominally a princess, Lala has no obvious responsibility or role as such. She only acts like a powerful ruler when she is suffering from a personality-warping virus in the twenty-fourth episode, and even then she is only acting on Rito's behalf. In the series finale her passivity and powerlessness are in stark contrast to Rito's heroism, as rather than stopping her father's planned destruction of earth herself, she instead waits for Rito to arrive and save the day. Just as the princess's status as 'protagonist' is taken away by the sleep forced on her in fairytales, Lala ultimately relinquishes the role of 'hero(ine)' and 'protagonist' to the male Rito.

The prince/princess dichotomy is not as clearly drawn in *The Melancholy of Haruhi Suzumiya*, but is implicitly referenced in the scene (discussed below) in episode fourteen where Kyon kisses Haruhi to 'save her' from her own power.

The 'Rescue'

In fairytales, the prince confirms his heroism and his superior status in relation to the defeated and impotent princess by 'rescuing' her. In the series finale *To Love-ru* explicitly draws on imagery from the fairytale *Sleeping Beauty* as Rito battles giant vines on his way to rescue Lala, held captive in her father's spaceship (castle). Breaking with fairytale convention, however, Rito does not battle alone but is reliant on the assistance of various female friends in order to accomplish his mission. One of Lala's female classmates qualifies this, saying 'But I'm a little jealous of Lala, having someone who is saving the world go to greet her like a prince on a white horse.' Even if women are able to take an active role, *To*

Love-ru demonstrates the assumption that, at heart, they still desire the passive role. In contrast, in *The Melancholy of Haruhi Suzumiya* Haruhi takes explicit objection to this, declaring the active 'princely' role much more desirable: 'If you just wait for something interesting to happen, nothing will', and decides that through her actions she 'declares to the world that [she is] not a woman who just waits around' (episode thirteen).

The Kiss

The kiss is the climax of the fairytale narrative, marking the prince's 'rescue' of the princess from her slumber and the commencement of their sexual relationship. In *To Love-ru* Lala briefly takes on the personality of a powerful ruler when she is infected by a personality-changing virus in the twenty-fourth episode, but is 'cured' and reverts to her former passive, submissive state when Rito declares that he loves her. Similarly, in *The Melancholy of Haruhi Suzumiya* Haruhi exercises her power to create a new reality, which she is shown enjoying before Kyon persuades her to renounce it by kissing her (episode fourteen), an act which makes explicit reference to the stories of *Snow White* and *Sleeping Beauty*. His decision to kiss her is informed less by his own desire for her (as he prefers Asahina) and more because the other members of the SOS Brigade have been giving him hints about how to curtail her power. As Kyon and Haruhi kiss, Haruhi's new reality is shown melting away, and Kyon is congratulated by the SOS Brigade for restoring the status quo; the world that existed before the female exercised her power.

Kyon and Koizumi, the two male members of the SOS Brigade, frequently state their opposition to Haruhi's creation of a new world and resolve that Haruhi must never learn of the existence of her own powers. Their fear is that of men unwilling to lose the existing system which benefits them in exchange for a new world, where women both realise and exert their own power. Haruhi herself is a symbol of the modern girl, whose dissatisfaction with the current social order leads her to defy it, only for her to be manipulated by men back into the existing patriarchal social system through the promise of love and a heterosexual relationship. This is essentially the subtext of all fairytale romances, where the kiss of a prince and all it symbolises (marriage and childbirth) awakens Sleeping Beauty and Snow White from their dreamland and re-embeds them in the patriarchal, heteronormative world of reality. This has been sold to women (and men) as the 'rescue' of women, using the persuasive power of 'romance' through media such as fairytales. That these fairytales have come to be perceived even by women themselves as the ideal in heterosexual gender relations shows that 'romanticism is a cultural tool of male power to keep women from knowing their condition' (Firesmith 1970, quoted in Hamilton 1978: 100).

Both *To Love-ru* and *The Melancholy of Haruhi Suzumiya* contain pornographic and romantic narratives. *To Love-ru* in particular is typical of much boys' manga, with its female characters serving primarily as wish fulfilment or 'fan service' for its (presumed) male audience. The women in *To Love-ru* are either willing to indulge the sexual and romantic fantasies of their male classmates or are powerless to resist them. This is comforting for the male viewer in that it presents a type of woman whom they are unlikely to meet in real life: simple, unthreatening, docile and not only completely subservient but happy to be so. In contrast, *The Melancholy of Haruhi Suzumiya* contains some sexualisation of women but is more self-aware. It engages with the romantic narrative in ways which construct familiar positionings of male and female, prince and princess, active and passive, but also is somewhat atypical of boys' anime in its depiction of the lead, Haruhi. Haruhi's dominant personality, expressed through her unilateral leadership of the SOS Brigade and her boisterous, self-assured behaviour, are a refreshing change from the usual female protagonist. However, the male Kyon repeatedly expresses his opinion that her independence and dominant personality make her unattractive to him, and traditional formulations of feminine appeal are reasserted in his love interest, Asahina. It is Haruhi, though, who is the 'princess' in *The Melancholy of Haruhi Suzumiya*'s fairytale narrative, and who is kissed by the 'prince'. In conclusion we can say that, while *To Love-ru* may perpetuate depictions of women as infantile sexual objects in boys' manga and anime, *The Melancholy of Haruhi Suzumiya* presents a more ambivalent depiction, both endorsing and problematising normative gender constructs.

To Love-ru and *The Melancholy of Haruhi Suzumiya* contain primarily pornographic and romantic narratives, and their typicality for that genre of manga and anime has been discussed above. However there are many boys' manga series which do not follow these narratives. Many manga may contain references to romance, or sexual motifs (such as the ubiquitous 'up-skirt shot'), but depict gender primarily in reference to other narratives. *Demon Detective Neuro Nōgami*, discussed below, is an example from the 'detective story' genre, and its depictions of gender are primarily tied to a criminological narrative.

DEMON DETECTIVE NEURO NŌGAMI

Demon Detective Neuro Nōgami is a manga series written and illustrated by Matsui Yūsei that ran in *Shūkan Shōnen Janpu* from 2005 until 2009. The series was adapted into a twenty-five episode anime series which aired from 2007 to 2008. I will be using the original manga series as my reference, as only this was available to me.

Female high school student Katsuragi Yako meets the titular Nōgami Neuro when her father dies under mysterious circumstances. Neuro reveals to her that, although he has adopted a human male form, he is really a creature from a magical reality who feeds on the energy released when mysteries are solved. Having exhausted the supply of mysteries in the magical world, he has come to the human world to solve them, starting with the death of Yako's father. Appreciating Yako's ability to interact with others, Neuro decides to use her as a figurehead detective while he solves mysteries to ensure that his true identity is not compromised. Yako is at first reluctant, but soon becomes determined to be of positive use to Neuro.

The series is initially episodic, with each individual case spanning two to three chapters. The latter half of the series, however, is dominated by longer story arcs culminating in a climactic final battle. The series is narrated almost exclusively from Yako's point of view, and while Neuro is the titular character, Yako is the real protagonist of the series and quite literally provides it with its human heart.

Narrator, Detective and Crime-fighter: Yako

Male-oriented series narrated by female characters are highly unusual; while girls often gender-cross and identify with male leads, the reverse is far less common as it entails a downgrade of social status and a loss of power (Allison 2006: 151). Yako is obviously female, perennially clad in her skirted high school uniform, but she has short hair, no curves and loose-fitting clothes that do not show off the sexualised areas of her body. There are no voyeuristic close-ups of her body; in fact she is often shown in super-deformed form and with her eyes bulging, on the receiving end of some sort of physical abuse from Neuro (see Fig. 2). The use of the extremely cartoonish super-deformed style is used to humorous effect and suggests that she is not intended as a sexual object for the reader's consumption.

Fig. 2: Yako is depicted 'super-deformed' and in an unflattering, unfeminine manner (Matsui Yūsei 2009).

Yako embodies stability and emotional intelligence, stereotyped as 'feminine' traits. Her embodiment of these is not necessarily negative, however, and the emphasis is less on her as the female counterbalance to Neuro's male, as the human to his non-human. Although there is a high number of female criminals, most of Yako's friends throughout the manga are adult men, who are variously non-human, violent or emotionally damaged. Even when they realise that it is Neuro who primarily solves the mysteries they still converse almost exclusively with Yako, recognising her importance to the agency. Godai, the detective agency's part-time helper, refers to Neuro and Yako together as 'the monsters' (*bakemono-domo*), and categorises their individual abilities as follows:

> I reckon the real one to watch out for is the one in charge (Yako). She'll fearlessly come and peer into your deepest emotions. Want to try being scrutinised by the detective (Neuro) from the outside, and the assistant (Yako) from the inside?

The criminal Asia Aya sums up Yako's gift succinctly, saying that while Neuro solved the *modus operandi* of her crime, 'you solved me as a person' (*anata ga watashi jishin o toita*). Neuro's ability to dissect the *modi operandi* of crimes is complemented by Yako's burgeoning ability to dissect the criminal's motive and mentality, a talent which becomes crucial as the series progresses. When the computerised entity HAL reveals that the password which will defeat him can only be gleaned by an understanding of his creator's psychology, Yako alone possesses the emotional insight necessary. She ultimately deduces the right password and defeats HAL, prompting him to admit 'If my opponent had only been Neuro, I was confident it wouldn't turn out like this. Yako Katsuragi ... it seems like your existence was beyond my calculations.'

Over the course of the series Yako, unusual for a female character, undergoes a process of self-improvement reminiscent of male sports anime. The chronicling of her personal growth also provides an overarching structure for the entire manga. Initially reluctant to play even the role of figurehead, her role as Neuro's puppet is symbolised in the pose she strikes before announcing the culprit; while still ignorant of the culprit's identity she allows her arm to be controlled by Neuro's magic and pointed at the criminal. Called a 'totally powerless marionette' and a 'puppet', Yako begins to worry about her passive role: 'I guess I'm just a puppet after all. There's nothing I can do that Neuro can't.' This pessimism soon changes to determined optimism, however, as she realises that although she does not possess Neuro's magical powers, she can still contribute. Neuro himself recognises Yako's potential early on, listing her with the female criminals Asia Aya and X (discussed below) as the three humans whom he sees as having the potential to transcend the boundaries of normal human ability.

Yako's growth is not without hurdles, as near the end of the series she breaks down, screams and cries upon witnessing the deaths of two friends, and quits the detective agency. She soon overcomes her own fear, however, and rejoins Neuro, declaring 'I won't run away any more, or snivel. There's something I need to do, something I need to see through to the end.' Manga heroines (of all ages) are often depicted screaming and crying when in danger. This breakdown is the only example of Yako doing so, despite her having witnessed various gruesome murders. This gives the impression of her as a strong, mature young woman, in contrast to the weak, infantile, prone-to-tears 'heroines' favoured by many manga. As Neuro's magical powers weaken towards the end of the series, Yako's active involvement is increasingly required, culminating in Neuro sending Yako alone into battle against the fearsome serial killer XI, telling her: 'Through all the incidents we have encountered, you should have become strong enough to compensate well for my getting weaker. You should be able to go ahead and exceed my expectations.' Successfully defeating XI, Neuro, who usually calls her 'slave' (*dorei*) signals his acknow-ledgement of her as an equal by addressing her as 'partner' (*aibō*). In the final chapter Neuro has returned to the magical world, and three years on from the events of the series Yako has become, in her own right, the world's greatest detective.

Demon Detective Neuro Nōgami can thus be regarded as a female coming-of-age story, as Yako searches for her own identity and worth as a detective and as a human being. She grows over the course of the manga, from Neuro's apprentice and (unpaid) assistant to a professional, confident young woman. The obstacles she meets she overcomes through her own persistence. This is a path traditionally trodden by male protagonists, with female protagonists (such as Usagi in *Sailor Moon*) usually gifted with their powers by someone else. Yako is an unusual female protagonist and this series' unconventional depiction of female gender is furthered in its portrayal of the criminals with whom she interacts.

Gender and the Criminological Narrative

On discovering that a serial bomber is a woman, Neuro warns Yako not to be shocked, stating that when it comes to crime 'sex is irrelevant' (*seibetsu wa kankei arimasen*). In reality, however, this is not true. In Japan, as in the rest of the world, the vast majority of criminals are male, and crime itself, as a social construct, is conceptualised as belonging to the 'masculine' sphere. Even within the field of criminology there remains a tendency to assume crime is male by default, only excepting those crimes which are committed most often by women (such as attacking or killing an abusive husband), or which are defined by 'feminine' (i.e. sexual or non-aggressive) characteristics (see for example Chesney-Lind and Pasko 2004). Declaring that biological sex and crime are unconnected, *Demon Detective Neuro Nōgami* is radical in presenting not only a higher ratio of female criminals to male than exists in reality, but also in the types of female (and male) criminality it explores.

Feminist criminologist Sandra Walklate claims that studies show that 'women will engage in the same kind of criminal behaviour deriving the same kind of pleasure and excitement from it as their male counterparts' (Walklate 2004: 7). However, since femininity and aggression are considered antithetical by hetero-patriarchal society, in both fiction and reality the capacity of women to commit murder is often 'neutralised' by reshaping the narrative to place her in the role of the victim. For example a woman who commits a crime in partnership with a man (often the husband) is portrayed as being brainwashed by him, or having done it out of love. The usual view taken by the courts, the media and the public is that 'men rape and murder, women watch and help with the clean up' (Morrissey 2003: 153). Essentially '[t]hese portrayals repeat traditional and "safe" positionings of male power and female passivity rather than explore the radical and threatening potential for new models of female agency' (Morrissey 2003: 24–5), and perpetuate the gender-crime divide.

Those examples of female criminality which cannot be excused or neutralised are portrayed as monstrous. Here the woman is again denied agency – although her action is acknowledged, she is no longer considered 'human' (Morrissey 2003: 24–5), let alone 'female'. In contrast, as aggression, violence and crime are ascribed to masculinity 'violence is viewed as one of many possible behaviour patterns for men' and 'when a man kills he can expect that his crime will be both imaginable and possibly even human' (Morrissey 2003: 17). The social acceptability of male crime is evidenced by the vast amount of fictional and real male crime narratives articulated, debated and even glorified in the popular media (Morrissey 2003: 17).

Feminist legal theorist Bronwyn Nalor sums up the discrepancy between media representations of male criminals and those of female criminals thus: 'Whilst male deviance is seen to exist on a continuum, female deviance is polarised: madonna/ whore [...] Snow White/the Wicked Queen' (cited in Morrissey 2003: 16). The author of *Demon Detective Neuro Nōgami*, however, has created a wide range of characters who do not adhere to the traditionally prescribed gender-differentiated criminal narratives. The female criminals portrayed engage both with gender and sexuality issues debated in modern-day Japanese society and with deeper, universal concepts of crime as a human, rather than a male, behavioural pattern. Each of the women discussed below deviates in some way from normative ideals of femininity such as chastity, sexual passivity and social docility, but adheres to other ideals such as motherhood, physical attractiveness and hetero-sexuality. It is the contrast between these traditionally feminine and non-feminine aspects which makes them interesting characters. They engage with and subvert feminine ideals, reflecting ambiguities on the part of the writer about traditional tropes of femininity and the role of women. The reason that *Demon Detective Neuro Nōgami* was not as broadly popular or commer-cially successful as many other *Shūkan Shōnen Janpu* titles (and not yet considered to merit an English translation) is perhaps due to its novel and often visceral exploration of the darkness of women's psyches, something which the (male) consumer is unused to confronting, but the existence of which he fears.

The Sexual Sadist: Genuine

In the latter half of the series the main villain Sicks is introduced, along with his vanguard of psychopathic henchmen. Genuine is the only female member of the male Sicks' vanguard, and is their commander (although she in turn follows Sicks' every order). Of the vanguard, she alone attacks Neuro without taking hostages, displaying a more aggressive and 'honourable' battle style than her male counterparts. She is also the only criminal in the entire series who, despite being initially defeated in battle against him, ultimately and successfully rebels against Neuro's control over her, prompting him to admit that 'she has defeated me'.

Genuine appears young, Western and exaggeratedly buxom, always clad in revealing low-cut dresses. However there are no close-ups on eroticised parts of her body, and rather than presenting her as a sexual stimulant for the (male) reader, her physique is used instead to underscore her personality as a sadist. She is frequently depicted standing on male slaves who wear blindfolds and S&M-style bondage gear, and while there is no indication that she has sexual relationships with any of them, she enjoys making them kill each other by promising to love the survivor.

Her sadism is explicitly explored as her defining charac-teristic. On the one hand, by emphatically tying together her sadism (fundamentally a sexual deviance) and her criminality, Genuine plays into the stereotyped role of 'female criminal as sexual deviant'. This trope is common to anime, and succinctly summed up by Napier: 'Women can be powerful, but the most powerful ones are clearly evil, and their evil is concentrated in their sexuality' (Napier 2001: 72). The assumption, only recently challenged, that men are inherently 'masculine' and women are inherently 'feminine' means that male crime and female crime have long been considered two separate phenomena, the first born out of normal 'masculine' aggression and the second born from some 'deviant' lack of femininity. There is still a global assumption that female crime occurs primarily when women stray from their culturally ascribed gender role, most often in the form of 'deviant sexuality' (Walklate 2004: 31). Genuine's crime is thus 'explained' by her sexuality; traditional 'femininity' (submission, sexual repression and masochism) and crime remain mutually opposed, and the gender concepts of the patriarchal society remain stable.

On the other hand, by placing her in the position of 'sadist', Genuine occupies a (sexual) role not often allowed to women in fiction or reality. This is weakened, however, by her taking on of a submissive, masochistic role first in relation to Sicks, then to Neuro. There would seem to be an underlying assumption, therefore, that for a woman to take on a controlling, sadistic role she must be exercising it on behalf of a man.

The Female Sexual Deviant: Ezaki Shiho

Ezaki Shiho is introduced in the manga as an attractive young woman who briefly expresses heterosexual attraction to her male university teacher, a character named Harukawa. A few pages later, however, she is shown butchering him. Although her transformation from student to murderess is due to Harukawa's 'electronic drug' (a computer-based virus which brings to the surface people's latent criminality), it is stressed that the drug did not 'create' her criminality. The reader is thus confronted with a rather attractive heterosexual girl drooling as she describes the excitement she feels when she stabs people:

> The feeling of pleasure in that moment when your body penetrates someone else's insides!! The feeling of pleasure that comes from knowing you have complete control over them!! [...] It really excites me [...]. What HAL (the computerized virus) woke within me was this desire to stab, this desire to penetrate.
>
> (*Tanin no tainai o jibun no karada ga tsuranuita shunkan no kaikan!! Aite o kanzen ni shihai shita to iu akashi no kaikan!! [...] mechakucha kōfun shita wa [...]. HAL ni kidukasareta no wa shisatsu ganbō, kantsū ganbō*).

The sexual aspect of her criminal desire is blatant, and it is a 'male' desire in as much as she wishes to be the penetrating, controlling, killing party, rather than the female penetrated, controlled and killed. After (non-fatally) shooting Neuro, the sexual dimension is once again stressed through her choice of words: 'Ah ... that's amazing [...]. Neuro, a lovely hole is opening up' (*aa [...] saikō [...] ii ana aiteiru wa, Neuro*). She is later defeated by Neuro and Yako.

Ezaki's desire to penetrate might be explained as 'masculinity' stemming again from her deviance from hetero-normative gender roles, but although she has entered 'masculine' areas of sexually motivated murder, this is at odds with her 'femininity' as previously indicated by her professed heterosexuality. As an example of female criminality this is ultimately more unsettling for the reader, as it opposes the cultural norms of patriarchal society and shows female criminality existing outside of the usual stereotypical models. This representation encourages a reassessment of the relationship between women and violent crime, and shows a female image which, in its violent defiance of traditional submissive femininity, reflects a very real fear of male society.

The Murderous Mother: Histerrier

The serial bomber Histerrier presents a juxtaposition of violent, aggressive criminality and the role of the mother and housewife, still revered in Japan as the pinnacle of 'womanhood' (Lock 1996: 77, 84). Her appearance as a young, attractive mother holding her baby is juxtaposed both by her words and the grotesque depiction of her, snarling and with canine features, when she switches into 'Histerrier' mode. She repeatedly expresses her desire to *'bucchakeru'*, meaning 'to let everything out' or 'to express oneself freely', and explains:

> I can't express myself! I can't show my true face in front of my family! I want to act out this impulse to kill! I can't help wanting so badly to destroy! In front of my family I have to be a good wife and a kind mother [...] I think everyone in the world is like me. For their happiness and that of the people around them, they live suppressing the one part of themselves they most want to express.

Histerrier uses the word *'honnō'*, which is translated here as 'true face' but really means 'instinct', and stresses her animalistic side. It is written using the kanji 本能 but the furigana (pronunciation guide) given in the manga read as カレ (*kare*) or オレ (*ore*), meaning 'he' and 'I' (both refer to men) respectively. This perhaps indicates an assumption that crime is automatically gendered male, and that it is easier to take on the role of 'criminal' as a woman if one renounces one's own womanhood in favour of a male identity.

Fig. 3: Histerrier switches between the face of a caring mother and that showing her animalistic instinct (*honnō*) in *Demon Detective Neuro Nōgami* (Yūsei Matsui 2006).

Histerrier's claim that she feels repressed by her family reflects Japanese social realities, where women are still largely ascribed to roles in the home and have more limited options than men for self-expression in social, political and employment-related areas (World Economic Forum 2012). While talking, Histerrier switches between shouting maniacally, her face distorted into a canine snarl, and reassuring her crying child with her features back to normal. She gets out of sync, however, and turning to her baby yells 'Shut up! Keep your mouth shut when people are talking!' (*Urusee! Hito ga shaberu toki wa damatte kikeyaa!*), hinting that her true anger might be with the child which has bound her further into the restrictive role of motherhood (see Fig. 3). Her use of masculine pronouns could then suggest that it is in particular those aspects of her nature which society deems 'masculine', including but not limited to her destructive criminality, that she feels are being repressed.

Her use of the pseudonym 'Histerrier', while playing on the concept of her as a 'dog' following her instincts to kill, also carries the additional meanings of 'terror' and 'hysteria'. 'Hysteria' in particular is a malady thought, from the time of the ancient Greeks to the early twentieth century, to be caused by the womb. Even now it continues to be considered an overwhelmingly 'female' condition (Gherovici 2010: 41, 48). Its symptoms are generalisable as an exaggerated emotional state but defy specification or enumeration; rather, as a pathologisation of female sexuality by male doctors, hysteria's symptoms are 'unconditionally faithful to the cultural mandates in place at any given time' (Gherovichi 2010: 56). Feminist academic and medical writer Rachel Maines decries hysteria as a sexist construction which serves to effect 'the reduction of female sexual behaviour outside the androcentric standard to disease paradigms requiring treatment', and points out that there is no corresponding masculine word to describe out-of-control irrationality (quoted in Gherovici 2010: 49). Like many women before her, then, Histerrier's murderous 'hysteria' was perhaps borne from her own female nature, or rather from the discrepancy she experienced between perceived societal and familial demands on her in terms of gender role fulfilment on the one hand, and her own animalistic human (rather than 'female') nature on the other. This character, then, is novel in its depiction of a violent, aggressive woman who is simultaneously fulfilling the 'feminine' role of mother, but this progressiveness is perhaps weakened by the choice of name which ties into sexist discourse blaming women's 'irrational' behaviour on their own womanhood.

The Ruthless Career Woman: Asia Aya

In the manga, Asia Aya is a globally-renowned singing star with the power to manipulate the human mind through song. She finds, however, that her power to connect with other people's minds diminishes when she is in love with someone. Therefore, to guarantee the loneliness which is the key to her success, she kills those she loves. Aya is the only criminal who, having been put in prison, continues to play a recurring role throughout the series; Yako goes to Aya for advice about her work with Neuro, and the two become close friends. Aya is depicted with considerable sympathy and as possessing 'normal' humanity (as opposed to Histerrier or Ezaki Shiho's manic criminal delirium), despite her cold-blooded murders. The choice she faces between maximising her talent to pursue a career and letting her talent die in order to experience love is an exaggerated representation of the situation of many real-world Japanese women, who still have little opportunity to possess both a career and a family simultaneously. That Aya chooses 'career' rather than 'family' and is still depicted (primarily through the means of her ongoing friendship with Yako) as a woman, and as a human makes her a subtly radical presentation of a female criminal.

The Androgynous Serial Killer: X

X is the pseudonym of a murderer whose motivation is to find out her or his own identity by examining the physiological make-up of others. Possessing a genetic ability to take on the appearance of any other human being, X cannot remember anything about her or his true identity, including whether he is in fact originally a 'he' and what his real name is. When not assuming the identity of someone else, X takes the form of an androgynous youth, his body hidden under a loose-fitting sheet. X is initially assumed to be male, uses the masculine '*ore*' when speaking in the first person, and is referred to using male pronouns by the other characters. X's true identity, however, is the female-gendered clone of the male villain Sicks. Upon learning this, X (now adopting the moniker XI) takes on a more female appearance with long hair and larger eyes, and is referred to using female-gendered third person pronouns. Before XI dies, however, she reverts back to being 'X', believing that that was in fact her *true* identity, even if it was not her *original* identity. In this way, while not explicitly engaging with transgender discourse, XI/X transcends the binary male/female gender divide and exemplifies a criminality which exists independently of physiological or mental gender.

Conlusion

Demon Detective Neuro Nōgami depicts both woman as hero and woman as criminal in the context of its detective narrative. I argue above that the protagonist Yako, in particular, represents a progressive depiction of an anime female in that, while reasonably attractive, her physical features are not considered 'important' by the other characters or by the author. Most noticeably, there are no sexualised depictions of her for either the reader or the other characters' enjoyment. Instead the focus is on her development as a professional, and she interacts with both men and women in a confident, self-assured and platonic manner. This makes her an unusual type of protagonist for a male-oriented series written by a man – as the main character and possibly the only 'relatable' (or 'normal') character, it is with her that the audience is encouraged to identify.

The criminals whom Yako and Neuro face are also novel in their depiction of varied female criminality. Criminals such as Genuine evoke associations between criminality and deviant sexuality which are part of a normative discourse privileging heterosexual gender roles, but Ezaki Shiho and Histerrier represent an interesting combination of socially desirable 'feminine' traits (such as heterosexuality, physical attractiveness, reproductive capacity and so on) and murderous, sadistic, animalistic desire. I argue that these characters are ultimately highly progressive for boys' manga in that they make the (male or female) reader confront their own preconceptions about gender roles and the wishes and desires of women, while refusing to deny these murderous women their 'womanhood'.

GINTAMA

The final narrative I examine is a humorous narrative. Many anime, even if not primarily comedic, contain elements of humour. This humour is often physical, as the cartoon style lends itself to exaggerated and fanciful occurrences. The series *Gintama*, however, is a comedy series which features mostly verbal humour. In both Japan and the West the number of women involved in producing, writing or delivering comedy remains low and jokes that target women are rife (for example jokes at the expense of another person's mother or one's own mother-in-law). *Gintama* is interesting in that its women are often the source, rather than the target, of the joke. The relationship between humour and comedy is explored in greater detail below.

Gintama is an ongoing manga and anime series. The title is written with the characters 銀魂, meaning 'silver soul' but the pronunciation plays on '*kintama*', a slang word for testicles. The manga has been published in *Shūkan Shōnen Janpu* since 2003, and as of 2010 it had been collected into thirty-two volumes which had sold in excess of thirty million copies (*Mainichi Shinbun* 2010). An anime adaptation numbering two hundred episodes was broadcast on TV Tokyo from 2006 to 2010 which followed the manga very closely, and I shall be using both as my reference.

Gintama is set in a fictional Edo[3] roughly twenty years after Japan's invasion by aliens. The setting is simultaneously historical, modern and futuristic. The Bakumatsu-era Shinsengumi[4] remain the police force in *Gintama*'s Edo, but they drive futuristic hover-cars. The citizens dress in traditional Japanese attire, but use modern-day products such as the internet, TV and karaoke

---

[3] Edo was the name of the Japanese capital until it was renamed 'Tokyo' in 1868.
[4] The Bakumatsu was the name given to the final years of the Edo period under the Tokugawa Shogunate, roughly corresponding to 1853–1867. The Shinsengumi were a special police force during the Bakumatsu period.

machines. The setting itself is thus somewhat 'incongruous', providing a perfect background for the incongruity-based humour which I shall discuss below.

The protagonist is the unconventional samurai Gintoki, who runs an 'odd jobs' shop with his two helpers, Kagura and Shinpachi. He is first introduced in the anime running away from battle, and despite his frequent acts of heroism he is just as often presented engaging in empty bragging and posturing with his rival Hijikata, satisfying his 'non-masculine' craving for sweet food with strawberry milk and chocolate parfaits (the hanging scroll above his desk reads 'sugar content' (*tōbun*)) or lazing about at home picking his nose and reading *Shōnen Janpu*. His helper Shinpachi is the 'straight man' of the series, an idol-obsessed teenage boy who is regularly irritated by Gintoki's irresponsible behaviour. Gintoki's other helper Kagura is a girl of about ten or twelve years of age who is a member of the Yatō, an alien warrior race. She has superhuman strength and is a fierce fighter, but in contrast to the rest of her clan she has the mental strength to control her desire to fight, declaring 'I decide my own battlefields myself'. She often joins Gintoki in his absurd behaviour, and her surprisingly foul mouth and uncouth behaviour are a frequent source of comedy.

Gintama contains strong elements of science fiction, historical parody and action, but is essentially a comedy series. The structure is molecular, with each episode constituting a stand-alone narrative. Occasionally there are longer story arcs, with some comedic stories lasting two to three chapters or episodes, and several serious action-based arcs covering approximately five episodes which differ noticeably in tone from the rest of the work. In their attempt to create pathos through invocation of existing social texts (such as a mother's self-sacrificing love for her child) these serious arcs often express stereotypical, heteropatriarchal assumptions about gender roles and lack the subversive power of the comedy episodes. The majority of *Gintama* is comedic, however, and I shall discuss below the presentation of gender in the context of its humorous narrative.

Gender and the Humorous Narrative

Japan scholar Reginald Blyth described women as 'the unlaughing at which men laugh' (cited in Finney 1994: 2). Yet *Gintama* provides an example of women not only escaping being 'that at which men laugh', but acting and speaking to place *men* as 'that at which men *and* women laugh'. Comedy and the carnivalesque provide a rich site for the study of gender at a more (self-)conscious level, yet have been overlooked by many academics. The comedy of *Gintama* combines physical and linguistic humour with social parody, and frequently breaks the fourth wall to engage in metafictional debate with the viewer about the series itself and other media or social issues. Much of the humour arises from repeated incongruities through script opposition – the juxtaposition of two or more concepts which, when combined, are humorous in their contradiction (Simpson 2003: 37–8). In *Gintama*, a social norm, such as a socially prescribed gender role, is often combined with an act which contradicts that norm to comedic effect. In this way the comedic structure itself serves to destabilise the existing social order.

Marguerite Wells, prolific writer on Japanese humour, presents the argument that parody and farce constitute only a fantasy release of aggression where at the end everything is as it was before, and so are less socially significant forms of humour. In contrast, satire is seen as more destabilising, as aggression is awakened in the viewer against real objects, and it is intended to bring about a permanent change in reality (Wells 2006: 209). In the following I argue that while it may lack the aggressive bite of satire, the playful parody of *Gintama* is able to subtly express the same message. While parody may reinforce the status quo by failing to bring about any permanent change, in *Gintama* parody is used so extensively as to destablise gender assumptions throughout, and there is no final didactic return to normality from the fantastical Edo it presents. Just because its humour is not aggressive, this does not mean it has no point to make or that it is unable to convey that point with the same force. I suggest that the humorous devices used in *Gintama* can be broadly categorised into physical humour, linguistic humour and parody, and these are discussed in turn below.

Physical Humour

'Physical humour' in the context of manga often means nudity, usually that of the female characters, and either unintended by them or unintentionally witnessed. In *Gintama*, however, there is only one instance of female nudity; a naked goddess appears before the male Shinsengumi members Kondō, Hijikata and Okita, only for the latter (as policemen) to arrest her for indecent exposure. A deadpan Hijikata covers her up with his jacket, remarking 'It's the middle of winter, aren't you cold?' In contrast, there are numerous depictions of male nudity, with the male body presented as something impure and inherently comedic – its display is always used to comedic effect, and is often referenced with diminutive and insulting language.

Importantly, as when the nude female is embarrassed by the gaze of others, male nudity in *Gintama* is disempowering. It is presented as comedic rather than sexual, resulting in some public humiliation or physical punishment, usually at the hands of a disinterested female protagonist. For example, when Kondō asks his love interest Otae to nurse him, she instead shoves a leek up his rear and makes him stand naked outside in the cold. The Gintoki-obsessed female character Sacchan similarly punishes the male Hattori Zenzō for distracting her when she is tending to Gintoki by shoving various objects into his rear end. On paper these punishments might read as sexualised, but the act itself is never shown – there is a sudden jump from the female character's look of anger or annoyance to a shot of the male's pitiful aftermath, meaning that the comedic aspect of their ridicule is much more evident. Those characters most regularly shown naked are also those presented as the least sexually attractive – Kondō is regularly

the butt of scatological visual comedy, while Hattori's haemorr-
hoids are a running gag, suggesting that their nudity is not intended
to be viewed sexually by the reader or the other characters. Gintama's nudity is thus purely comedic, dismissing the pornographic
motifs of *To Love-ru* or *The Melancholy of Haruhi Suzumiya*.

Linguistic Humour

The most popular model of linguistic humour in Japan is 'word-
bounded rhetoric', which plays on the meanings and sounds of
words already raised in the discourse (Takekuro 2006: 94). The
Japanese language has a relatively small number of phonemes and
a high number of homonyms, so perhaps inevitably puns are the
most common form of joke in Japan (Nagashima 2006: 76).

Gintama also uses the '*boke* and *tsukkomi*' style of humour
exemplified by Japanese *manzai* (a type of stand-up comedy),
where one person plays the idiot (*boke*) and the other the straight
man (*tsukkomi*). Essentially, the *boke* talks in an absurd or
unconventional manner, while the *tsukkomi*'s job is to correct and
criticise the *boke*, acting as the voice of social convention in
ridiculing his absurdity (Stocker 2006: 61). When this comedic
mode is used in anime and manga, female characters usually play
the *boke* or are excluded from the joke altogether; they cannot play
the *tsukkomi* due to the globally-held and long-standing myth that
women are somehow inherently 'unfunny' (Finney 1994: 1–2). In
Gintama, however, female characters frequently take the *tsukkomi*
role, while the men are often relegated to the *boke* role.

Much of the humour of *Gintama* comes through mis-
appropriated and 'gender-inappropriate' language, often delivered
by women. This allows women to break out of the restrictive model
of 'feminine speech' and opens up language as a gender-neutral
space for equal play. 'Feminine speech', as it is socially
constructed, is polite, entailing more extensive use of the polite and
honorific forms than male speech. It is naïve, in that not just the
language women use is restricted, but also what they are allowed to

discuss: explicit or sexual matters, common sources of humorous material, are considered inappropriate. It is also submissive, which is antithetical to the aggressive, confident nature of the joketeller or the critical *tsukkomi*. Japanese society's restriction of women's access to language thus reveals 'the workings of linguistic and cultural ideologies in the structural oppression of women' (Yukawa and Saito 2004, cited in Okamoto and Shibamoto Smith 2004: 8), and has denied women access to 'the joke'.

Fig. 4: Otae, dressed in a feminine flower-patterned kimono, wields a pike and yells 'Oi!!' (*uraaa!!*), her face twisted into an un-ladylike expression of anger (Sorachi 2004).

Much of the humour in *Gintama* derives from the incongruity between how one knows 'proper' Japanese women *should* speak, and how the female characters are *actually* speaking. Not just *what* they are saying but also *who* is saying it, and how, is comedic.

This incongruity is epitomised in Otae, whose depiction as a young, beautiful, perennially kimono-clad Japanese woman belies her rough, aggressive, 'masculine' speech. She frequently yells 'oi!' (*koraa!*) and 'goddamn!' (*konchikusho!*), uttering phrases such as 'don't fuck me about' (*fuzaken ja nai wa yo*) with a menacing grin and a sugary-sweet voice (see Fig. 4). This use of incongruity calls attention to socially normative concepts of 'feminine speech,' while eliciting comedy by its playful violation of them.

The contradiction between the idol Otsū's cutesy outward appearance and her use of (often scatological) language is also a source of comedy. Her affectation of a *shiritori*-style manner of speech (adding a word or phrase onto the end of every sentence leading off from the last syllable) is a parody of real-life Japanese idols who affect bizarre speech patterns as a motif or catchphrase. In Otsū's case, her *shiritori* utterances are always unrelated and nonsensical obscenities. Thus she urges the public:

At this time when everyone's getting carried away, make sure to lock your doors and watch out for terrorists – sell me your kidney you bastard!!

「浮かれちゃうこんな時期こそ戸締まり用心テロ用ジン臓売らんかいくそったれやぁぁぁ！！」

(*Ukarechau konna jiki koso tojimari yōjin tero yō-jin-zō uran kai kusottare yaaa!!*)

Everyone, just because it's spring doesn't mean you can get carried away – the elephant's crap is really big!

「皆、春だからって浮かれてじゃダメだぞうさんのうんこめ
っさデカい！」

(*Minna, haru dakara-tte ukarete ja dame da zou-san no
unko messa dekai!*)

Her songs are melodically the standard factory-produced pop fare
but the lyrics are shockingly obscene, mostly obscured by
censorship bleeps. Song titles include 'Your father is [censored]'
(*Omae no tōsan XX*) and 'Eat shit, civil servant!' (*Chomekō nanza
kuso kurae!*).

The young female Kagura frequently takes on the role of
tsukkomi and ridicules the idiocy of the men around her in
explicitly sexual terms, making fun of male sexuality and marking
the male genitalia as an object of comedy and contempt. The male
Shinpachi's horror at the idea of the female Kyūbee getting a sex
change operation: 'Are you saying she's going to construct a
corrupt tower of Babel!?' is met with Kagura's *tsukkomi*: 'You say
"a corrupt tower of Babel", but you've all got 'em.' When in a
particularly surreal story arc Gintoki's member is replaced by a
screwdriver, Kagura comments 'Gin-chan's thing has always been
a stick with no use. Better that it rotted and fell off', and later
reiterates her contempt, saying 'it's got no use except for peeing in
the street'. Elsewhere the male member is referred to as a
screwdriver, an analogue stick and a 'dirty antenna', and in this
way the male phallus becomes a comical object rather than a
weapon, and a source of ridicule rather than power.

Parody

'Incongruity is a binary relationship, it presupposes the presence of
a norm, which is then infringed [...]. One has to establish the norm
before one can violate it' (Simpson 2003: 41). By evoking certain
stereotypes, e.g. 'the ideal anime heroine', or 'the sexy (anime)
female', *Gintama* briefly engages with these conventions before
subverting them through parody, reducing them to a comedic
rubble.

In one episode, thinking that Kagura has left forever, the three supporting female characters Otae, Sacchan and Catherine compete to replace her as the female lead. Three male characters (Gintoki, Shinpachi and Hasegawa) decide to judge the candidates themselves, stating that 'from us guys' point of view, a heroine must fulfil three conditions: these are her face, her style, and her character'. Hasegawa explains that by 'style' he basically means breasts; 'from the moment you see them, it doesn't matter if you can't remember her face. If men's pervy gaze stays fixed on them even if they swing to the right or the left, that's a heroine [...] She needs a sexy body'. As discussed previously, this reduction of female worth to her breasts and sex appeal is common to boys' manga, as is the implicit power men have to decide what is 'attractive' in women by unilaterally designating them as an object of sexual desire or dismissing them as such. Although the three contestants do not explicitly object to taking part in this sexist competition, they manage to 'inadvertently' subvert the format. When asked to show their crying face, Otae 'misunderstands' and instead beats Hasegawa until he cries, while his attempt to appraise Otae's body results in her punching him in the face. Ultimately the men are too scared to choose between them so the women beat all of them up, and go to brawl it out by themselves.

Another episode where a socially sanctioned gender norm is established only to be obliterated through increasingly absurd parody features the female characters attending a cooking class. The trope of cooking as an important signifier of femininity was discussed above in the context of *To Love-ru*, and here Shinpachi echoes Rito's conservative assumptions that all women will get married and that a wife is obliged to cook for her husband. However, unlike Lala, Kagura reduces their conversation to the level of the absurd, stating with an expression of complete seriousness 'I'm not going to be a wife. If I was, I'd like to be Colonel Sanders' wife. That old guy has got those chickens completely under his control'. The other girls attending the cooking class are also engaging with the stereotype of 'cooking as an expression of one's love for a man'. The objects of their affection, however, are ridiculous; Kyūbee seeks to wed Ronald MacDonald, while Sacchan is after 'Kōmon's rectum', a joke which plays on the fact that Kōmon (the titular protagonist of the long-running Japanese period drama '*Mito Kōmon*') and 'rectum' are homonyms in Japanese. This sort of *reductio ad absurdum* is utilised frequently in *Gintama*, and entails focusing on a social or human attitude and magnifying it to chaos, in the process revealing its ridiculous nature (Mast 1973: 6). Thus rather than being a portrayal of traditional femininity and gender role fulfilment, the episode instead spirals into an absurdist parody of the stereotype.

Also targeted for parody are the sanitized, unrealistic expectations of women's physicality held by many modern-day Japanese men (which can be seen as a result of the proliferation of digitised and computerised female bodies in the mass media):

Shinpachi: 'Otsū doesn't fart or poop! Everything comes out as cute little eggs, like a quail!'

Kondō: 'Do you think you can maintain her purity like that? It's actually more disgusting. Even idols fart and poop! Face up to reality, you idiot!'

Shinpachi: 'So you're saying that my sister farts too?'

Kondō: 'Of course she does, and I accept that part of her too. Only in Otae's case, pink smoke comes out.'

This explicit referral to the bodily functions of beautiful women is an 'incongruity', at least in the sanitised world of anime. In *Gintama*, however, the female characters are frequently shown engaging in the same 'disgusting' behaviour as the male characters. Kagura is proudly declared 'the first heroine to vomit in *Shōnen Janpu*'s history' when introduced to the viewer, and is variously shown forcing herself to vomit, picking her nose until it bleeds, wiping snot on Gintoki's hair, and engaging in a burping contest with Gintoki and Shinpachi.

Men's preferences in pornographic and pseudo-pornographic manga are parodied in Sacchan, who expresses sexual desire but is never made into a sexualised object vis-à-vis the male characters or the consumer. Despite her good looks, her repeated attempts to get Gintoki to take advantage of her inevitably fail. Sexual submission is usually considered a marker of passive 'femininity' and thus desirable in a woman, but Sacchan's 'submissiveness' is exaggerated: she announces herself a masochist, begging Gintoki: 'Despise me, that's what turns me on!' (*motto sagesumeba ii ja nai, sore wa watashi o kōfun saseru no!*), and openly states that she has a fetish for bondage. In contrast, the male characters rarely express sexual desire, and Gintoki's normal reaction to Sacchan's advances is 'Shut up, you perverted woman!' (*omae wa damattero, hentai onna!*).

Conclusion

The female characters in *Gintama* often appear to wield more power than the men – Kagura's super-strength and Otae's aggression mean that both are far more useful in a fight than the other member of the Odd Jobs Gin-chan business, Shinpachi, or Gintoki's perennially down-and-out friend Hasegawa. Their position within the comedy set-up is similar – both frequently take the *tsukkomi* role, especially when belittling men who make any sort of sexual reference. Their disdain for male sexuality, and the portrayal of the male characters as the butt of the joke, places them in positions of power relative to the males. The male characters of *Gintama* are unable to sexualise them, and any attempt to do so results in the humiliation or physical punishment of the male characters instead.

The audience, similarly, is not granted any sexualised view of the females as they are rarely presented in ways that are conventionally attractive, with no nudity or close-ups of their erogenous zones, and frequent reference to their baser bodily functions. It is only the males against whom nudity is used, not primarily to sexualise (given the presumed heterosexual male audience), but to mock. Their nudity, often at the hands of females, renders them pathetic and vulnerable. This is in contrast to the majority of boys' manga where it is the female who is rendered naked and powerless at the hands of the male. *Gintama*, through its comedy, depicts women who are powerful yet caring, aggressive yet friendly, ill-mannered yet loved, and ugly yet respected. In short, it depicts female characters who are ambiguous, complicated, and human.

CONCLUSIONS

A survey conducted by the National Institute of Population and Social Security Research in 2005 of never-married Japanese people aged 18–34 found that 52 percent of men and 45 percent of women had no relationship with the opposite sex, romantic or platonic. These proportions held steady at least as far back as 1987 (cited in Tachibanaki 2010: 120). In a society with so little contact between its young males and females, it is unsurprising that boys' manga reflect a lack of understanding about the opposite sex, and a consequent ambiguity of presentation.

To Love-ru is perhaps the most conventional in its depiction of women, and the blatant sexualisation of women and their eagerness to be subordinate to the sexual whims of men are reminiscent of many boys' manga and anime series throughout the past few decades. It does, however, contain some moments where gender roles are called into question or not played out as typically expected – especially in Rito's lack of self-confidence when it comes to exerting his sexual dominance over the object(s) of his desire.

Yet while depictions of males in romantic anime may have become more diverse, allowing alternative masculinities, the females of *To Love-ru* remain one-dimensional mirrors of male desire, and perpetuate through their presentation the sexualisation, pacification and subordination of women. *To Love-ru* is a series which is unlikely to have many female fans, and the representations of women it transmits are rather troubling in that the male audience, many of whom may have little experience interacting with women in real life, are being poorly educated about the sexual and romantic behaviour that women will expect of them in reality. Of course, the audience will be aware that *To Love-ru* is a cartoon and not a very true-to-life one at that, but taken in the aggregate, the abundance of these representations of women in male-oriented popular culture may not only be informed by popular imaginings of women, but also exert a reciprocal effect on Japanese male youth's views regarding women.

The Melancholy of Haruhi Suzumiya goes some way to questioning the gendered assumptions unchallenged by *To Love-ru*, but its independent heroine is undermined somewhat by her incorporation into fairytale tropes. Moreover, the neutralisation of her powers by the fairytale narrative is not problematised, even though this series does make some 'tongue-in-cheek' comments about the presentation of women in anime. A female protagonist who is more radically questioning the characteristics expected of women in manga and anime is found in *Demon Detective Neuro Nōgami*, where Yako combines the best stereotypes of femininity (such as emotional intelligence and kindness) with the traits typically shown in male protagonists (courage, emotional strength and intellect).

Demon Detective Neuro Nōgami is also the only one of the four series discussed here where the reader is expected to identify with the female: in *To Love-ru* events are presented largely through Rito's point of view; in *The Melancholy of Haruhi Suzumiya* Kyon narrates his thoughts throughout, and in *Gintama* the main character is Gintoki. This is unusual for boys' manga, and may explain why this series was never as popular as many other *Shūkan Shōnen Janpu* titles, with far less merchandise available in stores, far fewer fan comics (*dōjinshi*) and no scheduled English translation as yet. Its depiction of female criminality is also unusual and interesting, forcing the reader to engage with a side of the female that is perhaps discomforting.

Finally, *Gintama* again has multiple female characters who play active roles in the construction of the series' jokes, often exerting their comedic power over the male characters by making men, and especially male genitalia (the source of 'maleness'), the butt of the joke. *Gintama*'s men and women are well fleshed-out characters embodying the contradictions which are integral to human nature: its male lead is a fierce soldier who nevertheless runs away from battle, while the female character Otae is a hostess who is frequently in trouble at work for beating up male patrons attempting to flirt with her. In *The Melancholy of Haruhi Suzumiya* gender roles are questioned but ultimately there is a 'return to normalcy' when Kyon establishes dominance over Haruhi by kissing her. In *Gintama*, there is no such normalcy to return to; that is, typical gendered power imbalances never exist in the world of *Gintama*, and so cannot be re-established. The fantastical, carnivalesque and totally unrealistic world of *Gintama* is perhaps the most accurate (or at least the most progressive) portrayal of the balance of power between men and women in the real world of all the series discussed here. This surely goes some way to explaining its popularity with female consumers (evidenced by the large amount of *dōjinshi* produced for it). It remains, however, popular with males also, and this should be viewed as evidence that a boys' manga series does not have to resort to sexualised or one-dimensional fantasies of women in order to gain readers, but may instead depict women who do not necessarily adhere to the anime ideal.

The series discussed above present but a tiny fraction of the myriad narratives challenging, reaffirming and subverting tropes of gender and sexuality in boys' manga works, but the varied and often contradictory gender ideologies underpinning the depictions of women in the four series discussed provide some insight into the Japanese male's ambiguous engagement with notions of gender. Recent years have seen the exploration of many new gendered narratives in boys' manga, encouraged by shifting social attitudes and consumer trends, which depict women in ways that mitigate, problematise, ignore and reject gender stereotypes about 'femininity'. *Gintama*, *Demon Detective Neuro Nōgami* and (to a lesser extent) *The Melancholy of Haruhi Suzumiya* are strong examples of that trend. *Gintama* and *Demon Detective Neuro Nōgami* demonstrate that popular series can feature women in prominent roles in narratives that are not related to sex or love – the women in these stories are not just defined through their relationships to male characters.

I conclude that this is evidence of a progression in boys' manga towards new and more realistic depictions of women, which reflect and hopefully promulgate a better understanding on the part of Japanese males of the opposite sex, and an acceptance of women as equals. A caveat to this conclusion must be added, however, with the recognition that series such as *To Love-ru* and *The Melancholy of Haruhi Suzumiya* likely will continue to be popular with Japanese males. The conceptions of women reflected in and fostered by such manga and anime represent a more reactionary attitude towards women, which sees their worth primarily as sexual objects and submissive domestics, and their presence only necessary to comfort, reassure or sexually excite the male characters and the male viewer.

REFERENCES

Allison, Anne (1996). *Permitted and Prohibited Desires: Mothers, Comics, and Censorship in Japan*. London: Westview Press.

Allison, Anne (2006). *Millennial Monsters: Japanese Toys and the Global Imagination*. Berkeley: University of California Press.

Amano Masako (1984). 'Onnatachi no 'sei' to 'sei': sei kankei no mirai' (The gender and life of women: The future of gender relations), Joseigaku kenkyūkai (eds) *Kōza joseigaku 1: Onna no imēji* (Womens' Studies Seminar 1: The image of women). Tōkyō: Keisō Shobō, pp. 74–101.

Anime News Network (2006). 'Japan's Favorite TV Anime'. http://www.animenewsnetwork.com/news/2006-10-13/japans-favorite-tv-anime (accessed 3 November 2012).

Bishop, Beverley (2005). *Globalization and Women in the Japanese Workforce*. Abingdon: RoutledgeCurzon.

Chesney-Lind, Meda and Lisa Pasko (2004). *The Female Offender: Girls, Women, and Crime*. Thousand Oaks: Sage.

Clammer, John (1995). 'Consuming Bodies: Constructing and Representing the Female Body in Contemporary Japanese Print Media', Lise Skov and Brian Moeran (eds) *Women, Media and Consumption in Japan*. Richmond, Surrey: Curzon Press, pp. 197–219.

Eisenstein, Zillah (1998). *Global Obscenities: Patriarchy, Capitalism, and the Lure of Cyberfantasy*. New York: New York University Press.

Finney, Gail (1994). 'Introduction: Unity in Difference?', Gail Finney (ed.) *Studies in Humor and Gender, Volume 1: Look Who's Laughing: Gender and Comedy*. Langhorne, Pennsylvania: Gordon and Breach Science Publishers, pp. 1–16.

Freedman, Alisa (2002). 'Commuting Gazes. Schoolgirls, Salarymen, and Electric Trains in Tokyo', *Journal of Transport History* 23/1, pp. 23–36.

Genz, Stéphanie (2009). '"I Am Not a Housewife, but…": Postfeminism and the Revival of Domesticity', Stacey Gillis and

Joanne Hollows (eds) *Feminism, Domesticity and Popular Culture*. New York: Routledge, pp. 49–64.

Gherovici, Patricia (2010). *Please Select Your Gender. From the Invention of Hysteria to the Democratizing of Transgenderism*. New York: Routledge.

Hamilton, Roberta (1978). *The Liberation of Women: A Study of Patriarchy and Capitalism*. London: Allen & Unwin.

Harris, Cheryl (1998). 'A Sociology of Television Fandom', Cheryl Harris and Alison Alexander (eds) *Theorizing Fandom: Fans, Subculture and Identity*. New Jersey: Hampton Press, pp. 41–54.

Henshall, Kenneth G. (1999). *Dimensions of Japanese Society: Gender, Margins and Mainstream*. Hampshire: Palgrave Macmillan.

Langton, Rae (2009). *Sexual Solipsism*. Oxford: Oxford University Press.

Liddle, Joanna and Nakajima Sachiko (2000). *Rising Suns, Rising Daughters*. London: Zed Books.

Lock, Margaret (1996). 'Centering the Household: The Remaking of Female Maturity in Japan', Anne Imamura (ed.) *Re-Imaging Japanese Women*. Berkeley: University of California Press, pp. 73–103.

Mainichi Shinbun (2010) 'Gintama: maeuri tokuten dai ni dan wa 'makie shiiru' Gintoki, Katsura-ra goshu Meiji Nyūgyō to no korabo mo'. (Gintama: The special gifts with preordered copies of the second DVD are a variety of five lacquered stickers of Gintoki, Katsura et al.; special collaboration with Meiji Milk). http://mainichi.jp/enta/mantan/news/20100221 mog 00m200036000c.html (accessed 22 March 2010).

Mast, Gerald (1973). *The Comic Mind: Comedy and the Movies*. Second edition. London: New English Library.

McLelland, Mark J. (2000). *Male Homosexuality in Modern Japan: Cultural Myths and Social Realities*. Richmond, Surrey: Curzon Press.

Miya Yoshiko (1994). 'Sekkusu wa jinkaku to kirihanaseru ka: Poruno ronsō', Inoue Teruko, Ueno Chizuko and Ehara Yumiko (eds) *Nihon no feminizumu, volume 6: Sekushuariti.* ('Can one separate sex from personality: Debating pornography', Japanese feminism, volume 6: Sexuality). Tōkyō: Iwanami Shoten, pp. 238–254.

Morrissey, Belinda (2003). *When Women Kill: Questions of Agency and Subjectivity.* London: Routledge.

Nagashima Heiyō (2006). '*Sha-re*: A Widely Accepted Form of Japanese Wordplay', Jessica Milner Davis (ed.) *Understanding Humor in Japan.* Detroit: Wayne State University Press, pp. 75–84.

Napier, Susan (1998). 'Vampires, Psychic Girls, Flying Women and Sailor Scouts', Dolores P. Martinez (ed.) *The Worlds of Japanese Popular Culture. Gender, Shifting Boundaries and Global Cultures.* Cambridge: Cambridge University Press, pp. 91–109.

Napier, Susan J. (2001). *Anime from Akira to Princess Mononoke: Experiencing Contemporary Japanese Animation.* New York: Palgrave.

Okamoto Shigeko and Janet Shibamoto Smith (2004). 'Introduction', Okamoto Shigeko and Janet Shibamoto Smith (eds) *Japanese Language, Gender and Ideology: Cultural Models and Real People.* Oxford: Oxford University Press, pp. 3–22.

Reynolds, Richard (1992). *Super Heroes: A Modern Mythology.* London: B.T. Batsford.

Saitō Minako (2001). *Kōittenron: Anime tokusatsu denki no hiroin zō.* (One woman amongst men: The presentation of heroines in anime, science fiction and biography). Tōkyō: Chikuma Shinsho.

Schodt, Frederik (1996). *Dreamland Japan: Writings on Modern Manga.* Berkeley: Stone Bridge Press.

Simpson, Paul (2003). *Linguistic Approaches to Literature, Volume 2: On the Discourse of Satire – Towards a Stylistic Model of Satirical Humor.* Philadelphia: John Benjamins.

Stocker, Joel (2006). 'Manzai: Team Comedy in Japan's Entertainment Industry', Jessica Milner Davis (ed.) *Understanding Humor in Japan*. Detroit: Wayne State University Press, pp. 51–74.

Tachibanaki Toshiaki (2010). *The New Paradox for Japanese Women: Greater Choice, Greater Inequality*. Translated by Mary Foster. Tōkyō: International House of Japan.

Takahashi Takako and Tsushima Yūko (2006). 'Female Sexuality and the Male Gaze: A Dialogue Between Takahashi Takako and Tsushima Yūko', Rebecca Copeland (ed.) *Woman Critiqued: Translated Essays on Japanese Women's Writing*. Honolulu: University of Hawaii Press, pp. 119–145.

Takekuro Makiko (2006). 'Conversational Jokes in Japanese and English', Jessica Milner Davis (ed.) *Understanding Humor in Japan*. Detroit: Wayne State University Press, pp. 85–98.

Toku Masami (2007). 'Shojo Manga! Girls' Comics! A Mirror of Girls' Dreams', Frenchy Lunning (ed.) *Mechademia 2. Networks of Desire*. Minneapolis: University of Minnesota Press, pp. 19–33.

Tokuhiro Yoko (2009). *Marriage in Contemporary Japan*. Abingdon: Routledge.

Ueno Chizuko (1994). '"Sekushuariti no kindai" o koete' (Overcoming 'modern sexuality'), Inoue Teruko, Ueno Chizuko and Ehara Yumiko (eds) *Nihon no feminizumu 6: Sekushuariti*. (Japanese feminism 6: Sexuality). Tōkyō: Iwanami Shoten, pp. 1–37.

Ueno Chizuko (2006). 'Fuan na otokotachi no kimyō na "rentai": Jendāfurii basshingu no haikei o megutte' ('The strange "solidarity" of anxious men: about the background of "gender-free" bashing'), Ueno Chizuko, Miyadai Shinji, Saitō Takao and Kotani Mari (eds) *Bakkurasshu! Naze jendāfurii wa tatakareta no ka?* (Backlash! Why is 'gender-free' under attack?). Tōkyō: Sōfūsha, pp. 378–438.

Ueno Chizuko and Nobuta Sayoko (2004). *Kekkon teikoku: Onna no wakaremichi*. (Wedding empire: A woman's crossroads). Tōkyō: Kōdansha.

Wakakuwa Midori (2003). *Ohimesama to jendā: Anime de manabu otoko to onna no jendāgaku nyūmon.* (Princesses and gender: An introduction to Gender Studies for men and women learnt through anime). Tōkyō: Chikuma Shinsho.

Walklate, Sandra (2004). *Gender, Crime and Criminal Justice:* Second edition. Abingdon: Willan Publishing.

Wells, Marguerite (2006). 'Satire and Constraint in Japanese Culture', Jessica Milner Davis (ed.) *Understanding Humor in Japan.* Detroit: Wayne State University Press, pp. 193–218.

World Economic Forum (2012). *Global Gender Gap Report 2012.* http://www3.weforum.org/docs/WEF_GenderGap_Report_2012.pdf (accessed 12 November 2012).

Zenkoku Shuppan Kyōkai & Shuppan Kagaku Kenkyūjo (2007). *2007 Shuppan shihyō nenpō* (National Publishers Association annual publication index report 2007). http://ja.wikipedia.org/wiki/日本の漫画(accessed 12 December 2009).

Zenkoku Shuppan Kyōkai & Shuppan Kagaku Kenkyūjo (2008). *2008 Shuppan shihyō nenpō.* (National Publishers Association annual publication index report 2008). http://www.geocities.jp/wj_log/rank/ (accessed 22 March 2010).

Manga and Anime references

Gintama. [TV programme] TV Tokyo. 2006–2010.

Matsui Yūsei (2005 – 2009). *Majin Tantei Nōgami Neuro: volumes 1~23.* (Demon Detective Neuro Nōgami). Tōkyō: Shūeisha.

Sorachi Hideaki (2003 – 2009). *Gintama: 1~29.* Tōkyō: Shūeisha.

Suzumiya Haruhi no Yūutsu. (The Melancholy of Haruhi Suzumiya). [TV programme] Tōkyō MX. 2006, 2009.

To LOVEru -toraburu-. [TV programme] TBS. 2008.

3 Absent Fathers

Fatherhood in Moral Education Textbooks

Zoya Street

Supervisor: Brigitte Steger (2010)

Table of Contents

INTRODUCTION

While I was living in Japan in 2008–2009 I became interested in ethics and morality in Japanese culture. When I asked a co-worker on the cusp of retirement, 'What are Japanese morals?', he quickly took a piece of paper and wrote in beautiful, flowing calligraphic style the Chinese characters for loyalty and filial piety – central Confucian teachings about how you should relate to your superiors. The question of how to relate to one's father in particular is central to these teachings. However, as this dissertation will discuss, morality in relation to the father as taught in Japanese schools is not based on Confucianism. Many of my Japanese friends considered the lack of respect and loyalty Japanese women and children have for their husbands and fathers to be at the core of Japan's social problems. It was in this context that I became interested in how children are taught to relate to their fathers at school.

Japanese school children receive moral education classes of one hour per week throughout elementary and junior high school, between the ages of six and fifteen. The lessons cover topics such as friendship, bullying, cheating and prejudice (Higashi 2008: 43). In addition to the moral education classes, the Ministry of Education states that moral education should be incorporated in all other school subjects. Most studies on Japanese moral education have focused on how morality is imparted in school life as a whole. They have portrayed contemporary moral education as a rational tool for nation-building that teaches the Japanese to behave for the benefit of the group. Klaus Luhmer (1990) focuses on the way national identity is imparted through moral education. Brian McVeigh focuses on moral education as a rational, economic tool of the state, intended to reproduce 'existing politico-economic arrangements' (McVeigh 2004: 128) by 'bureaucratising subjectivity' (McVeigh 1998). Gerald LeTendre (1999) studies the way Japanese schools create complex hierarchical relationships between teachers and students in order to impart democratic ideals that depend on the maintenance of harmony and responsibility to the group.

I hope to show a different side of moral education. I do this by focusing on stories in moral education textbooks. In particular, I analyse the network of symbolic relationships that surround the portrayal of fathers in these textbooks in order to understand the moral purpose of the image of the father. When I began to study post-war Japanese moral education textbooks from the late 1990s I was shocked to find that the depiction of fathers had not changed in the 50 years since the subject was reintroduced into the school curriculum. As masculinity in Japan has been undergoing a seismic shift since the 'lost decade' of the 1990s (Dasgupta 2003: 131; Roberson and Suzuki 2003), this raises questions about why the portrayal of fathers did not change as society changed, so that it was more relevant to the audience. One possible explanation is that the textbooks were published not long after this change began, so their content had not yet been affected by this social change. However, it is also possible that the purpose of the stories is not simply to accurately represent a typical, contemporary Japanese family. The portrayal of fathers in the stories serves a morally instructive purpose and careful comparison of these stories enables us to draw conclusions about the way his role in moral education is perceived, rather than simply aiming to reflect a social reality.

In this dissertation I make two arguments. The first concerns selfhood, and stands in contrast with previous research as described above. My analysis of the textbooks finds that protagonists, and by extension the readers, are treated not as citizens, subjects or group members, but as self-motivated individuals. My second argument is that the way that fathers are portrayed in moral education textbooks promotes this individualised selfhood. The fathers in the stories encourage the protagonists to behave based on individual concerns.

Japanese moral education textbooks are usually anthologies of morally instructive short stories. They are not described as textbooks (*kyōkasho*) but as supplementary readers (*fukudokuhon*) to acknowledge the fact that morality is taught not just in moral education classes, but throughout the whole of school life. The moral lessons imparted in the textbooks are intended to reflect the contents of the education guidance materials (*Gakushū shidō yōryō*), a government-issued guide on how school subjects should be taught (Khan 1997: 136–137). They are compiled by special committees within textbook publishing companies.

In this dissertation I look at a sample of sixteen stories that feature a father figure, published between 1966 and 1996. Half of the stories I have used in my sample come from books in the Textbook Library in the Japan Textbook Research Center (*Kyōka-sho kenkyū sentā)* in Sengoku, Tokyo, and are intended for students in their first year of junior high school. I chose this age group primarily because it is slightly above the median age of students that receive moral education classes. Since the students are slightly older, the language used is fairly complex, allowing me to carry out detailed analysis of the content. Textbooks targeted at an older age group may be problematic because some ideas would be taken as understood from previous years' study and not explicitly stated. The remaining half of the stories come from *Minna no dōtoku* (Morality for everyone, 1989), a textbook I was given by a colleague. It is intended for students in their fourth year of elementary school.

Working with textbooks from different periods opens up two possibilities: a high correlation between theme occurrence and periods would make the evidence anecdotal, but would highlight historical change; a lack of correlation between theme and period would mean that my sources are a sample of one single dataset, increasing the reliability of qualitative analysis. When I arranged my semantic analysis mind-maps into a single chart, I found no historical pattern regarding theme occurrence. Therefore, in the analysis given below I treat my sample as a single dataset, because the depiction of fathers in post-war moral education textbooks did not change between 1966 and 1996.

I have given the stories numbers, rather than referring to them with their full title. Story numbers are composed of three parts: the publication date, the year group the textbook is intended for, and the story within that book. For example, 66.1.1 refers to a story called, 'My name', written for first year junior high school students, published in 1966. A full list of the stories analysed, their designated numbers and brief plot synopses can be found in the appendix.

I have used a technique called 'domain analysis', an ethnographic method devised by James Spradley for research into cultural meaning. Tacit cultural knowledge is unveiled by looking at networks of semantic relationships in a text. A 'domain' is a 'symbolic category that includes other categories' connected by specific semantic relationships (Spradley 1979: 100). This is done by looking for occurrences of a 'cover term', and searching for other terms or phrases that semantically relate to the cover term in the same way. The use of domain analysis limits the impact of my own pre-existing cultural associations in my examination of how fathers and other semantic categories are represented in Japanese textbooks and minimizes the influence of one's own stereotypes when analysing the texts. For example, when I read the word 'silent' (*damatteiru*), I may think that to be silent is to be miserable, angry, boring or emotionally distanced. I may even think my own interpretation is the obvious, standard one, and fail to recognise my own subjectivity. Domain analysis has the ability to reveal that many of our assumptions about the use of certain terms in a foreign culture, and by extension our assumptions about the culture itself, are mistaken.

I combined domain analysis with the open source mind-mapping software 'Freemind' (version 0.8.1) to visually represent the semantic relationships at play in stories that feature a father. While each story has its own mind-map representing the semantic relationships within it, I also consolidated these maps into one larger 'master map', which allowed me to see the relationships present in all stories in one document. I then rearranged the details on this larger mind-map into themes, and created smaller, separate maps based on them. This new application of domain analysis allowed me to visualise the contents of and relationships between the domains present in stories that feature a father, and also allowed me to see whether the occurrence of themes and techniques correlated with publication date.

A HISTORY OF MORAL EDUCATION IN JAPAN

Morality has had a prominent place in Japanese education for centuries. The position of the self in moral education varied depending on prevailing historical trends. The historical summary I give here will provide background information for my first argument concerning the role of selfhood in Japanese moral education.

In the Edo period, Neo-Confucian ethics formed a major part of a samurai's education in the elite *shijuku* (private academies) and *hankō* (fief schools) (Adams 1960: 61; LeTendre 1999: 286). These ideas centred around the observance of vertical norms in order to maintain social and cosmic order (Shimbori 1960: 97); in other words, knowing your place in the world and acting accordingly.

Such Confucian ideas were in many ways at odds with the liberal Western ideas that ordinary Japanese people began to have access to after opening to the West in 1853. The translation of books such as Samuel Smiles' *Self Help* (1869) created an influx of ideas that gave people a new way of seeing themselves and their lives. People were more inclined to see their place in the world based on an entitlement earned through learning and self-improvement, rather than determined by the rank they were born into (Gordon 2003: 103).

The Meiji educational system was designed to move Japan away from its feudal past towards an industrial future (Adams 1960: 61). This ethos is summed up in the phrase *bunmei kaika;* civilisation and enlightenment. Throughout the Meiji era there was tension among policymakers about how to achieve the balance between modernising the public by teaching them liberal ideals based on individualism, and ensuring social cohesion for the purpose of industrial production and economic advancement (Shimbori 1960: 97).

Mori Arinori, who was Minister of Education from 1886 to 1889, for instance had strong views on the necessity of moral education for the success of the extensive political reforms Japan had to undergo: 'A prosperous, happy and permanent republican government can only be secured when the people who live under it are virtuous and well-educated' (Mori 2009 [1871]: 14). He took inspiration from liberal political theorist Herbert Spencer, advocating a systematic, scientific form of education that would mould and restrain the human character (Swale 2000: 58).

Moral education classes, then called *shūshin*, were introduced in 1872 as part of the creation of a compulsory school system (*gakusei*). *Shūshin* is a Confucian term that literally means 'cultivation of the self'. The Chinese character used for self has a strong connotation of the material self or the body, so *shūshin* is about controlling and refining your behaviour. At first the subject was unregulated and taught at the discretion of teachers, although in 1873 the government recommended a list of textbooks, all of which were based on Western texts that often preached individual betterment through education (Marshall 1994: 31).

Mori and other Meiji politicians agreed that schooling should inculcate morality for the good of the state. However, they disagreed when it came to the implementation of these ideas. Fukuzawa Yukichi was concerned by the perceived failings of morality based on Confucianism, criticising it for 'a lack of the idea of independence' (Fukuzawa 1899: 215). By contrast, Motoda Eifu, a Confucian traditionalist, criticised the Western-inspired educational system in 1879 for having 'reduced benevolence, justice, loyalty and filial piety to a subordinate position' (Monbushō, *Gakusei 100 nenshi* 2: 7; quoted in Marshall 1994: 54). This debate expressed an ongoing struggle between the perceived need to modernise Japanese society by incorporating the ideal of individual independence and the desire to inculcate harmonious social values in the state education system.

As a compromise between these two views, in 1879 a vague, government-sanctioned syllabus was created in order to limit the perceived harm caused by the influence of liberal ideas and educate children on Confucian morality. Also included in the guidelines was a strong focus on reverence for the emperor as subjects within a modern state (Adams 1960: 61; Luhmer, 1990). In other words, the problems associated with modern individualism were resolved by a focus on the self as an imperial subject. In 1881 *shūshin* was made a major school subject, and came to occupy ten hours' teaching time a week. This time included the teaching of Japanese history and national identity (Khan 1997: 65). The 1890 Imperial Rescript on Education put at the core of the education system a combination of State Shinto, Confucian ideas about proper rela- tions with authority, and the modern political idea of people as 'subjects' of the emperor (Luhmer 1990). The document is addressed to, 'Ye, Our subjects,' and continues:

> [...] be filial to your parents, affectionate to your brothers and sisters; as husbands and wives be harmonious [...].
> (quoted in Gordon 2003: 105)

This established the centrality of family relations to moral behaviour, and hints at a continuum between the family sphere and the state as 'national family' (*kokka*). By hinting at this continuum between the private and national spheres, the family served a double function as a Confucian moral concern and symbol of modern citizenry.

Shūshin lectures instilled a sense that something greater than the individual exists, be it the nation or the emperor, for which one must in one way or another sacrifice oneself (Shimbori 1960: 97). There was no discussion, and no questions asked of the teacher (Oshiba 1961: 231). As a citizen, individual happiness should be pursued 'in tandem with the greater good' (*Gakusei yōryō* quoted in Swale 2000: 129).

The political uncertainty after the death of the Meiji Emperor in 1911 and the end of the First World War in 1918 brought more controversies over moral education policy. Liberal values regained popularity in some parts of Japanese society and were incorporated into lessons (Luhmer 1990). The Japan Teachers' Union Enlighten- ment Association, founded in 1919, dedicated itself to 'attaining a just life based on human rights [...], the basic rights of human beings and [...] their inalienable social rights', and opposed government-mandated curricula and textbooks. At the same time, the Ministry of Education further reduced material in its moral education textbooks that taught individualism, and increased the material on patriotism and the family in 1911 and 1918 (Marshall 1994: 106–7). After 1925, when military officers were assigned to all schools to oversee the nationalistic and military training of children, *shūshin* took on a militaristic tone (Luhmer 1990).

Due to *shūshin's* role in the militarisation of Japanese youths, it was suspended under the American Occupation in 1946. It was replaced by 'Social Studies' lessons, which were intended to give children the knowledge and skills required to make their own value judgments about their heritage and the rapid changes happening in their society (Adams 1960: 61). The 1947 Fundamental Law on Education (*Kyōiku kihon-hō*) stressed individualism, responsibility and independence, and in 1949 the Imperial Rescript on Education was officially revoked (Luhmer 1990). The Japanese were now to be taught to see themselves as individuals and not as imperial subjects.

Between 1953 and 1962 juvenile crime increased dramatically (Duke 1964: 189). Parents blamed the extended freedoms offered by this new social order (Adams 1960: 61). Many criticised the haphazard introduction of an American educational system (Oshiba 1961: 146). In their eyes, Japan had suddenly changed from a tightly circumscribed world based on loyalty and obedience to a materialistic, individualistic world with no traditional ethical moorings to keep it steady (Adams and Oshiba 1961: 18).

In 1958, just as in 1872, it was in the context of growing social disorder that the Japanese government re-introduced moral education to the school syllabus. The term *dōtoku,* meaning 'way of virtue,' was coined to replace the word *shūshin,* which had taken on negative connotations due to its militaristic content during and shortly before the war (Lanham 1979: 6). The course was voluntary, but teachers allied to the Japan Teachers' Union (JTU) boycotted it, opposing what was regarded as a step back to the pre-war nationalistic indoctrination by the government (Duke 1964: 186).

The opposition was based on a combination of ideological and professional factors. The JTU wanted to defend liberal, democratic principles in education and prevent the adoption of policies that, in their view, were being proposed by the same elements in government that wanted to rearm Japan. They were keen to also protect the position of teachers as experts on the needs of the children with whom they had a close, personal relationship (Shimbori 1960: 101). Many teachers pointed out that the informal day-to-day moral guidance they gave children was more appropriate for cultivating individuality than a pre-planned weekly lesson based on a curriculum written by the prefectural board of education (Adams 1960: 61).

The Ministry of Education on the other hand favoured the introduction of moral education classes. The argument of the JTU relied on the assumption that all teachers were skilled enough to integrate moral education into other courses – but a separate moral education curriculum, as well as obligatory teacher training in moral education, would make up for possible failings in this respect. Furthermore, the ministry argued that Social Studies and day-to-day guidance were sufficient for teaching empirical prob-lem-solving and ethical discipline, but inadequate to cultivate an inner self or teach children about their heritage (Shimbori 1960: 100). Although the need for greater social harmony was the main motive for reintroducing moral education, the arguments used to defend moral education centred on ideas such as 'inner self', rather than authoritarian ideas such as filial piety or loyalty.

Under the 1962 revision to the educational guidelines (*gaku-shū shidō yōryō*) weekly hour-long lessons on moral education were made mandatory (Duke 1964: 186). The suggested lesson plans included in the teacher's guide have been analysed by Benjamin Duke; then as now, the focus was on instructive stories, such as Fukuzawa Yukichi's diligent efforts to learn English or the indomitable spirit of Helen Keller (Duke 1964: 187). Far from being purely concerned with building up nationalistic feelings, foreign examples could also provide an ideal that Japanese children could pursue. There was one chapter on 'Love of the homeland', but this mostly focused on how children could play a role in helping Japan to change for the better and did not contradict the individualistic ethos of the Fundamental Law on Education. Students were to be taught freedom as well as discipline, self-government as well as self-control (Duke 1964: 188).

In the 1980s, Prime Minister Nakasone Yasuhiro set up an ad-hoc council on education (*Rinkyōshin*), which proposed changes to the Japanese education policy to further individuality, inter-nationalisation, information technology and lifelong learning. Although Nakasone's reforms were not fully implemented, these suggestions were picked up by the Ministry of Education later in the 1990s. At that time, the curriculum was slimmed down, the school week was reduced from six days to five, and students were given greater choice as to what subjects they would study, in order to achieve *yutori kyōiku* (relaxed education) and *yutaka na kokoro* (richness of mind/heart) (Cummings 2003: 31–36; Rose 2006: 132–133).

The topic of moral education resurfaced in Japanese politics in the mid- to late-1990s, as an expression of the moral panic caused by the sarin gas attack on the Tokyo subway in 1995 and a brutal murder carried out by a fourteen-year-old in 1997. At that time, many debates in the Diet centred around the perceived need for greater emphasis on the education of the heart/mind (*kokoro no kyōiku*). These debates eventually led to the dissemination of Ministry of Education-published workbooks called *Kokoro no nōto* (Notebook of the heart) to all elementary and junior-high school children (Rose 2006: 146). These are not textbooks, but workbooks for personal use, with many sections to be filled in by the students with their own stories and views (Horio 2003: 33). This measure has been highly controversial, partly due to a perception that they constitute nationalistic government indoctrination. The measure received large support from right-wing groups such as Atarashii

Rekishi Kyōkasho o Tsukuru-kai (Society for the Creation of New History Textbooks) and Nippon Kaigi (Japan Conference), who were campaigning for the revision of Japanese history textbooks with regards to the events of the Second World War and a rewriting of the Fundamental Law of Education to include clauses concerning morality and national identity (Rose 2006: 146). The Fundamental Law of Education was revised in December 2006 under Prime Minister Abe Shinzō.

Approaches to moral education in Japan have been forged in the context of opposing forces that have driven educational policies and practices since the Meiji period. While some policymakers and practitioners have prioritised freedom, self-improvement and modernity, other have pushed back in defence of traditional Confucian morality, nation-building and stability. Moral education, as practiced today, is a compromise intended to satisfy both polarities in Japanese educational thought.

APPROACHES TO MORAL EDUCATION TODAY

In this section I will outline some of the most important issues concerning selfhood in moral education in Japan today. First, I will argue that the role of authority figures such as teachers in Japanese education is not to teach subordination of the self to authority, but to enable the development of individual autonomy. Secondly, I will argue that while some scholars claim that 'sentimentalism' (*shinjō-shugi*) leads to a group-oriented, harmony-focused morality, sentimentalism can in fact be pragmatic and individualistic. Finally, I will explain that socialisation in Japan concerns the movement of the self through a network of ever-widening 'inner' and 'outer' circles.

Guidance and Authority

Teachers contribute to the moral development of their students during all classes (Arai, Inuzaka and Hayashi 2005: 30) using a method called guidance (*shidō*) (LeTendre: 1994). Brian McVeigh (1998) argues that *shidō* and moral education are instruments of the state, which 'bureaucratise subjectivity' in order to 'mobilise minds'. He emphasises the use of causative verbs (such as *saseru*, to make someone do something) when describing moral education in Japanese. Moreover, he points out the requirement to teach patriotism described in the guidance materials and analyses moral education as part of 'strategic schooling' geared towards 'maintenance of the state'. He sees moral education as an instrument of authority, designed to undermine people's ability to think for themselves and lock them into an authoritarian, statist structure.

McVeigh suggests that the use of causative verbs in the guidance materials implies coercion – teachers are to 'make students think' in a particular way. This is misleading, because causative verbs in Japanese do not necessarily denote a lack of freedom on the part of the agent. It can mean that the agent is enabled to carry out an action that s/he could not have done otherwise, thanks to the influence of the subject. This interpretation of the use of causative verbs is consistent with other theories on child development in Japan. Morality is considered to be transferred by quasi-osmosis from role models to the children in their care (Toyama-Bialke 2003). 'Osmosis' is not a process of forceful indoctrination, but the natural, effortless movement of moral knowledge, which occurs when a child spends a lot of time in close contact with a moral guide.

This idea is fundamental to the complex relationship between teacher and student. The leadership abilities of a teacher in Japan are seen as contingent on their close participation in students' lives. The teacher gains the gratitude and admiration of students through participation and service, for example by taking part in cleaning the classroom, which leads to a more egalitarian relationship, while it is still clear that the teacher is the leader (LeTendre 1999). This idealisation of a close, personal teacher-student relationship has historically contributed to the hesitation teachers have towards hour-long, weekly, planned moral education classes, which are seen as too impersonal (Shimbori 1960). This would indicate that *shidō* practices are not authoritarian in the statist sense that McVeigh describes, but function as part of a trusting relationship in which the teacher tries to help the students to find out by themselves what morally good behaviour would be in specific situations.

Conservative educational sociologists Arai Ikuo, Inuzaka Fumio and Hayashi Yasunari (2005: 24–25) argue that without the instruction of a teacher in moral values, a child cannot develop self-reliance. Arai, Inuzaka and Hayashi recognise the difficulty of maintaining individual freedom while at the same time teaching children to have a predetermined set of values. However, they claim that a teacher should be able to distinguish between ideas that are a product of current trends, and those which will continue to be important for the rest of the child's life. The content of moral education should focus on the latter. By focusing on timeless truths moral education can encourage children to decide for themselves how to behave, while still giving them instruction in desirable behaviour (Arai, Inuzaka and Hayashi 2005: 24–25). Therefore, individual autonomy is not necessarily compromised by moral education.

Sentimentalism

The Japanese Research Association for Social Studies [as a school subject] (Nihon Shakaika Kyōiku Gakkai 2000: 98–99), a research institute based at the University of Tsukuba, highlights three main approaches to the teaching of moral education. The first is moral essentialism (*dōtokuteki honshitsu-shugi*) which 'clarifies the essence of moral values and enables children to internalise these values'. Second is moral sentimentalism (*dōtokuteki shinjō-shugi*) which is based on the belief that 'moral sentiment leads to moral action'. The use of dramatic stories with a moral message – the sole content of moral education textbooks – is the main way of teaching such moral sentiments.

The final approach described is pragmatism, which 'combines scientific and moral thought, values and reality, knowledge and will'. The Association for Social Studies prefers pragmatism, arguing that moral essentialism breeds an internally inconsistent set of abstract values, and moral sentimentalism promotes behaviour based on harmony, and does not encourage the ability to discern for themselves what is right (*handanryoku*). Pragmatism, on the other hand, allows people to decide for themselves what is the most desirable result from a given situation and, accordingly, discern what behaviour is appropriate.

The implication of this is that moral education textbooks, which are almost entirely composed of stories, rely on the cultivation of moral sentiments and are therefore fundamentally unable to encourage the cultivation of individual autonomy. However,

Arai, Inuzaka and Hayashi offer a slightly different interpretation of the role of sentiment in moral education.

> You could say that sentiment (*shinjō*) is something like energy, and fixing that energy on a target is the ability to discern (*handanryoku*). The ability [...] to hit that target – in other words, to link your sentiment to concrete action – is described [in the educational guidelines] using words such as 'practical will' (*jissen iyoku*) [...]. (Arai, Inuzaka and Hayashi 2005: 31)

This interpretation of moral sentiment overlaps with moral pragmatism. Therefore, moral sentimentalism does not necessarily lead to indecisive behaviour that merely follows the will of the group. Moral education textbooks can teach individuality.

Socialisation and Circles

Socialisation (*shakaika*) is defined by Arai, Inuzaka and Hayashi as three different processes:

> Creating groups and societies.
>
> Changing reproduction and childrearing from a private affair to a public, collaborative affair.
>
> An individual, having been made to internalise social values from mutual relationships with other people, taking on a social existence [...]. (Arai, Inuzaka and Hayashi 2005: 39)

Once children begin their kindergarten and school education, childrearing becomes a public affair. Moral education is an explicit part of this. Points one and three are important in understanding how this is carried out – moral education textbooks fictionalise groups and societies such as the family and the individual, represented by the protagonist, takes on a social existence within these groups. This means that the textbooks are serving a socialising function in their approach to implementing moral education.

Transition from *uchi* towards *soto*

The distinction between *uchi* and *soto* is made clear in the controversial *Kokoro no nōto* (Notebooks of the heart). Part of the purpose of *Kokoro no nōto* is to provide teaching materials for moral education that focus on the role of the family and the local community in childrens' moral development (Egawa 2003: 121). The table of contents of the junior high school edition proceeds as follows:

'I am one member of a (more) important family.'

'I like this school.'

'Let's come to like our hometown more.'

'I love this country, I live in this country.'

'Let's think deeply (*omoi o haseru*) about the world.'

This represents a model used in Japanese moral education for children to relate appropriately to the world:

Love your family

Love your school

Love your hometown

Love your country

International contribution (*kokusai kōken*).

(Horio 2003: 33)

Familial relations are seen as a gateway to relations within ever widening circles, culminating in the development of positive internationalist attitudes. The connection of the family to the country in this series of widening circles may seem to be a worrying return to

101

the pre-war view of the state as a national family (*kokka*). How-ever, there are also differences. In the pre-war system the Emperor was seen as the 'father' of the national family, and Japan was portrayed as the natural leader of other Asian nations, while the more recent system lacks a leader figure or a supremacist narrative. Nevertheless, the passage of the self through the family towards wider society and nation appears to be a common thread in the history of moral education in Japan.

The series of widening circles mirrors the formula that has been used to organise the teaching requirements for Moral Education listed in the educational guidelines since 1988. The 1988 reform to the education guidelines was carried out with advice from Oda Yukio, a leading proponent of *kokoro no kyōiku*, who later wrote in 2002 that the development of a rich heart consists of a heart that is hard towards oneself, a heart that is kind to others, a heart that can be moved by beautiful things, and a heart that dedicates oneself to the society and the public good (quoted in Higashi 2008: 46).

This shows that the movement of the individual person between *uchi* and *soto*, and the portrayal of the world as a series of concentric social circles through which the individual person is always moving, are central ideas in Japanese moral education. Nationalism is not obviously a central goal of moral education. It goes without saying that learned moral behaviour for the benefit of oneself, the family and other social circles could easily be channelled into nationalistic goals as well. However, at least in the stories that deal with the father do not, the moral education textbooks do promote other values.

FATHERHOOD IN POST-WAR JAPAN

The second argument of my dissertation concerns the role of fictional father figures in the processes of socialisation and moral education described above. In this section I will give a description of fatherhood in post-war Japan, which will serve as the social background to my analysis of the model of fatherhood depicted in moral education textbooks.

The portrayal of fathers in diverse media and public discourses in Japan is heterogenous. There are three main images representing the father: the idealised past, when fathers received the proper respect from their families based on Confucian teachings; the dystopic present, when fathers are weak, dominated by women at home and by faceless bureaucracies at work; and the future ideal, when fathers might have more fluid working patterns and be more involved with childrearing.

In post-war Japan, the image of the ideal man has changed rapidly. The stereotypical Japanese salaryman, who works long into the evenings for his family, was the dominant ideal in the 1970s and 1980s. As John Traphagan and Hashimoto Akiko (2008: 7) point out, 'by the second half of the twentieth century the figure responsible for the wellbeing at home shifted quite noticeably from the father figure to the mother figure.' On the level of popular representations, the absent parent has been a dominant theme in dark *anime* as well, which expresses the isolation felt by the many young Japanese who have had little contact with their fathers (Napier 2008). Arai, Inuzaka and Hayashi write that the lack of authority fathers have at home is bad for the moral development of children, as it deprives them of the opportunity to rebel against an authority figure, and thereby takes away the impetus to fly the nest and become independent, contributing to the creation of what he calls 'moratorium people' (*moratoriamu ningen*; Arai, Inuzaka and Hayashi 2005: 165–166).

Economic and labour-market uncertainties since the 1990s have brought this previous ideal into question, with large numbers of Japanese young men rejecting the traditional image of masculinity in search of a more fluid lifestyle that allows them to spend more time on leisure activities and their families (Honda 2005; Mathews 2003). Moreover, due to the perception that the low birthrate is partly caused by women's reluctance to give up work to be the sole caregiver for children, the government has tried to persuade men to help more with childrearing. The Ministry of Health, Labour and Welfare has taken steps to make the workplace environment more conducive to childcare leave by providing grants for retraining, paid leave and financial aid to companies that offer paternity leave. The Sam Campaign by the Ministry of Health, Labour and Welfare attempted to promote 'hands-on' fathering, by promoting as a role model the husband of a famous pop star (Sam), who is the primary caregiver for their children (Roberts 2002).

As mentioned above, since the 1990s increasing numbers of Japanese young people have rejected the security and rigidity of a career as a salaryman. Instead of pursuing long, hard hours of salaried work, they engage in temporary, part-time work, often in the service industry. Additionally, many young people are without formal and permanent employment. Known as 'freeters' (*furiitā,* a contraction of 'free arbeiter', from the English word 'free' and the German word for worker) they depend on irregular work. In 2000 they numbered about four million, about half of these being willfully underemployed, while the other half reported that they were looking for stable employment. It is difficult to acquire regular, salaried employment after having been a freeter, as most employers only accept trainees who have just graduated from university (Honda 2005: 5).

Opting for the lifestyle of a temporary worker goes against the grain, but can perhaps still be considered masculine. However, this is a different sort of masculinity to the image of the salaryman. Freeters may be considered masculine if they pursue personal fulfilment through leisure activities, which is out of reach for the majority of corporate employees. Masculinity as self-fulfilment offers a way out of the dichotomy between the outdated salaryman masculinity and the unattainable, family-centred masculinity proposed by the Sam Campaign (Mathews 2003: 121). If increasing numbers of Japanese men opt for this lifestyle, social perceptions of masculinity are likely to change. When these men become parents, public perception of fatherhood might also change. This may cause the 'idealised past' image of fatherhood to become even more distant from the modern reality. On the other hand, since freeters and other irregular workers will have more time to spend with their children, this could lead to more active participation of some fathers in childrearing (see also Deacon's contribution to this volume).

There are therefore a number of different ways that fatherhood could be portrayed in late twentieth century Japanese texts. The fathers depicted in the stories I will analyse below should be considered not just on the basis of what they are, but also what they are not, because a decision to focus on one kind of father is a decision to exclude others.

Zoya Street

LANDSCAPES OF MORAL DEVELOPMENT:
THE CONTENT OF THE STORIES

In the stories which feature father figures there appears to be a deliberate differentiation between the home and places outside of the home. Events that take place within the home are set apart from events that take place outside of it by their fundamental narrative purpose. Outside the home, the protagonist encounters a new situation and transforms as a result of it (linear change). Inside of the home, the protagonist is challenged by his or her own behaviour and by the end of the story regains a pre-existing moral condition (cyclical change). This is made particularly clear in the concluding line of 67.1.1 when the father says, 'My son has returned to me,' even though the son did not physically go anywhere. Story 93.1.2 is also cyclical in nature; the father begins as a healthy and hard-working character, and the child starts the story as a happy-go-lucky character who enjoys working hard at school. Family life is disrupted by the father's sickness, but after his recovery everything returns to normal, and the child renews her understanding of the value of hard work.

The home as a narrative structure in moral education text-books is the scene for introspection and regaining one's innate qualities, while the world outside the home is where protagonists learn how to become a different sort of person. Leaving the home is a metaphor for learning to live in society, a concept expressed by the Japanese phrase '*seken ni deru*' (go out into society).

This separation between home and outside symbolises the separation between *uchi* and *soto,* the inner circle and the outer circle. In Japan, a child's first encounter with the *soto/uchi* distinction usually occurs in reference to the home (Hendry 1987: 39). The purpose of this separation in fictional stories represents the socialisation process of 'creating groups'. The group being created in this case is the family, represented by the home. The home and the family are symbolic of *uchi*, which encompasses one's private, internal psychology and also the relationships in which one can express one's true, inner experience, or *honne* (Hendry 1987: 40). Cyclical moral change that happens within the home is a renovation of one's internal psychology, specifically one's inherent moral qualities.

The daunting descriptions of the space outside of the home are an example of how children in Japan are often taught to associate *soto* with danger and fear (see Hendry 1987: 41). The challenges characters face in this daunting space cause a linear moral change, which they must undergo as part of the process of 'taking on a social existence'. In other words, this moral change entails acquiring the qualities required to live in the social world outside of the safety of the home. This creation of inner and outer groups strongly echoes *kokoro no kyōiku*, or education of the heart, which places the self, the home, wider Japanese society, and international society in ever-widening circles.

The space outside the home is portrayed as a challenging space outside of the child's comfort zone. In three out of four of the stories that cover a journey outside the home, the environment is described as dark, and the protagonist experiences powerful feelings of fear and nervousness. For example, in 89.4.2 the protagonist feels his heart beating rapidly, his cheeks become warm, and he thinks of himself as truly alone (*hontō ni hitori botchi*). The home can also be described negatively – usually little detail is given about the appearance of the home, but when there is some description it is 'destitute' (*binbō,* 89.4.2) or 'embarrassing' (*hazukashii,* 93.1.2). These descriptions occur in stories in which the father works hard to try to improve the lot of his family, so poverty is a necessary narrative device that highlights the im- portance of the father's role as a breadwinner. Furthermore, the emotional meaning of the home is described very positively, such as in 67.1.2 – 'your home is something that you miss dearly (*totemo koishii*) when you are separated from it.' Spaces outside the home are dangerous and frightening, while the home is something to which one is emotionally attached.

Places outside of the home are often the setting for a challenge. For example, in 93.1.1 the protagonist must leave the house to go to a stationery store to apologise for breaking a window, and in 89.4.2 the protagonist is sent on an errand to buy bread and bacon, but on the way loses the money she was given. Outside the home, characters leave their comfort zone and face dramatic, emotional challenges, and undergo an emotional transformation by facing that challenge and succeeding. In 89.4.2 the mother greets the child outside of the house to reassure her and give her more money, after which the child runs happily back to the shop (*genki ni kakedasu*). The mood of the child changed from upset and worried to relieved and happy, and the child learns to be more careful with money in the future.

The stories I have analysed always feature a challenge that the protagonist must overcome in order to become more moral. The father is strongly implicated in the setup of these challenges. In 89.4.2 the father, as breadwinner for a poor family, says to the mother, 'Argh, today this is all we have,' and hands over two silver coins. The child remembers this interaction after having lost one of these two coins, and it is implied that this is the reason for the child's strong emotions. In 93.1.5 the protagonist returns to Tokyo after visiting his hometown when his father reminds him of his obligation to the animals in his care – in other words, the father sends his son out to face the world. The protagonists thus face emotional challenges, expressed by the words of their fathers, in the world outside of the home.

Considering the need to 'create groups' in order to socialise children through moral education textbooks, such depictions of idealised father figures may have little to do with how fathers actually are in modern Japan. The textbooks' homogeneity in story structure and character depiction where fathers are concerned might be necessary in order to systematically construct an easily recogniseable family sphere. The structure and character of the family may act as a bridge between the individual and wider society. Likewise, the behaviour of the fictional father may be geared towards morally instructive lessons that are of use to life in the wider world, rather than an attempt to accurately represent the modern Japanese father.

By focusing on the theme of *uchi/soto*, or home and society, I have found that one role of the father is to initiate challenges that help the child to develop as a person. Depending on the setting of the story, these challenges either help the child to rediscover their own inner qualities or enable the child to acquire qualities that will allow them to live in wider society.

Behaviour and Characteristics of the Father

Despite the criticism of the absent or invisible fathers (*mienai chichioya*) in real life, father figures in moral education textbooks universally have little to do with everyday childcare. Their work often takes them far away from home, and they speak very little to their children. In contrast to this negative image of the distant father, fathers are depicted in moral education textbooks as quiet and often absent because they have a unique moral role to play that cannot be carried out by someone more talkative and affectionate. The distance and silence of the father gives him a clarity that allows him to guide the child to a better understanding of him- or herself, which eventually leads to stronger personal aspirations.

In the stories I have analysed there is a systematic relationship between the behaviour of the father, the development of a sense of selfhood and the drive to work hard. The distant but observant gaze of the father allows him to know the protagonist better than he or she knows herself, and based on this knowledge he gives insightful advice. The resulting self-awareness leads to personal ambitions and goals, which in turn motivate the protagonist to work hard.

The father often works away from home. For example, in story 93.1.1 the father works as a teacher in another prefecture, and his return home every Sunday is described as 'a time we really look forward to' (*totemo tanoshimi na toki*). Independent of whether they work away from home or not, fathers are often portrayed as men of few words (e.g. '*shizuka*' in 96.1.1 and '*damatteiru*' in 63.1.1). In story 67.1.2 the father works in a different prefecture for years, only returning home for the New Year holiday, and yet for the first year of his absence he does not write letters to his family because his handwriting is poor (*ji ga heta*). This adds even more emotional value to the letters he does begin to send after this first year has passed. In 96.1.1 the narrator describes a feeling of closeness towards his father that he had never felt before (*ima made nai chichi ni kinkan*), even though he is already in his mid-twenties when the events in the story happen, indicating that he felt distant from his father during his whole childhood.

The father, however, is not unkind, even if he is distant or quiet. In many stories that feature the father, a powerful, yet unkind adult male character appears as a contrast to the father. One example is Mr Yamauchi of story 93.1.3, a person the father remembers from his own youth, who, although being a person one really wants to emulate (*totemo akogare na hito*), cruelly tells the father that he is incapable (*omae ja muri da*). Similarly, *jiisama* (old man) of 93.1.1 is described positively as having strength of character (*kibone*), but is nevertheless very frightening, yelling at the protagonist, who believes that he will hit him. In the same story the father is described as kind most of the time, having never hit the child even once. The distance and silence of the father is therefore not to be confused with indifference.

Other examples show that part of the role of the father is to observe the child. In stories 93.1.5, 93.1.1 and 96.1.2 the father is described as watching the child carefully or quietly (*damatte watashi o miteiru, shibaraku me o mitsumeteita, mitsumeru koto ga ooi*). In 96.1.1 and 93.1.1 the father adjusts his posture to face the child properly, without speaking, and later again changes the way that he sits (*nani mo iwazu ni furimukau, muki-naoshita, suwari-naoshita*). In 63.1.2 the father almost never sees his children but by implication 'sees' them in dreams of his hometown.

The watchful gaze of the father is sometimes referred to as a form of communication in itself. Story 93.1.5 includes the phrase '*me wa kataru,*' meaning that the father's eyes tell a story even though his words do not – *wa* implies a comparison between the father's communicative eyes and his silent speech organs. Even story 93.1.6, which I present later as an exceptional case, includes a reference to the father advising his son by communicating through eye contact (*me to me de sōdan shita*).

Through this mindful observation he is able to discern accurately what the child is really thinking and feeling and how the child ought to behave. In 93.1.5 the father is described as knowing everything, whilst in other stories this quality is implied by the fact that he gives insightful, intelligent advice. In 93.1.1 the child tearfully admits to having broken a neighbour's window, and although the mother offers to apologise to the neighbour on the child's behalf, the father says that the right thing would be for the child himself to apologise for what he has done. The father's voice is described as quiet, with a low-level power (*shizuka; teiryoku*). This example shows that the emotional approach of the mother is sometimes considered inappropriate, and what is required for the child to learn a moral lesson is the distanced judgment of the father.

The idea that the father plays a role in the child's self-realisation and self-motivation is further supported by the fact that in stories 93.1.5 and 96.1.1, places such as the hometown and homeland are the site for deciding a person's future. In both stories the protagonists are young adult men at the start of their careers, following a personal ambition. In 93.1.5 the protagonist, a zoology graduate, returns to his hometown after failing the exam required to be promoted to a permanent staff member at Ueno Zoo, and one very brief, slightly cryptic utterance from his father, 'Your otters are lonely,' convinces him to return to the zoo and continue to work hard for the good of the animals in his care. The narrator describes his feelings in that moment as 'I sprung awake like a jack-in-a-box. My father's words pierced through my heart, exactly like a bolt of lightning.' In 96.1.1 the protagonist is a graduate of theatre studies and creative writing, and studied for his degree abroad in New York. It is after returning to Japan, and once again sharing a home with his father, that he decides to become a writer. This decision is described as '*hakkiri*', meaning bold, clear or definite and as a kind of *ikioikomu,* a verb meaning both to be excited and to brace oneself. These examples show the dramatic emotional power that protagonists feel as a result of the influence that fathers, particularly in the home environment, have on the protagonists' self-knowledge and motivation to work hard.

The behaviour of the father – his absence from the home and silence inside the home – creates a distanced relationship between him and his child which enables him to observe the child carefully. His absence and lack of attention to the child's everyday affairs is thus not something that should earn him criticism. On the contrary, based on this mindful observation, the father is able to give wise advice to the child and helps him or her to learn a moral lesson.

Selfhood and Hard Work

Stories that include father figures often portray a sense of self, that is, of identity and purpose in life. This is most easily seen in the regular use of words that include a *kanji* for self. In story 93.1.3 the father shares an anecdote from his youth and concludes by pointing out the importance of following your own path (*jibun no michi*) and finding a passion in life. This path and passion act as fuel that you can 'burn' in order to make yourself 'shine' (*jibun o kagayakaseru*) and to overcome yourself, in the sense of overcoming your weaknesses (*jibun ni katsu)*. In 93.1.2 the child is told to contribute to the household by wholeheartedly doing what she wants to do (*jibun ni yaritai koto o sei ippai ni yareba ii*).

The importance of selfhood in these stories is made clearer by the causal link between personal ambition and hard work or dedicated practice. This is exemplified most clearly by story 93.1.3, in which the cruel words of Mr Yamauchi remind the young father that baseball is something that he liked, that he wanted to become (*jibun ga suki na mono; jibun ga nareru mono*) and this gives him determination (*kesshin*) to practice. In 96.1.1, the child realises after an insightful anecdote from the usually silent, observant father that hard work leads to success.

The presence of another character for 'self' in words that indicate intensity of effort puts an interesting spin on the role of selfhood in hard work. In story 96.1.1 the study and practice are described on two separate occasions as *muga muchū*, which is a Buddhist term and means to lose yourself in something or be completely absorbed in it. The last two characters, *muchū,* can be used separately with the same meaning, and literally translate to 'in a dream'. The first two characters, *muga,* have been included because of their etymological link to selfhood. They mean selfless, self-effacing or self-renouncing. The character for 'self' here is *ga,* which has connotations of the untrained self. For example, the word, *wagamama* literally translates to 'the self as it is' and means 'selfish'. Hendry (1987: 44) gives *wagamama* as an example of what the Japanese consider an undesirable yet innate character trait that must be trained out of children. The use of the term *muga* implies that it is hard work to train out the self as *ga*. One can draw the conclusion that there must be a distinct difference between the self as *ji* (*jibun*) and the self as *ga* (*muga muchū*). Perhaps the presence of *ji* and the absence of *ga* lead to hard work. If so, the former must be more refined and desirable than the latter, which is selfish and undeveloped. This distinction does not seem to hold true for the phrase *jibun ni katsu* (to win against oneself), which describes the process of overcoming the flaws of *ga* fairly closely, and yet the word used for 'self' is *jibun.* However, it must be noted that the original phrase was *onore ni katsu*, a phrase that spread in youth education in the Meiji period and was used, for instance, when the young men had to go out in a winter morning, dressed only with one shirt to do so. The change from *onore* to *jibun* (both meaning 'self') might be because children today are no longer familiar with the term *onore* or because the writers of the textbooks intentionally tried to avoid a connotation of pre-war moral values, although, as anthropologist Peter Cave reports, some school clubs have banners displaying the original phrase (Cave 2004: 389–391, 412).

In story 93.1.3 the word *gamushara* is used, again to describe intensity of effort. The *ga* here is the same character for 'self' as described above. *Gamusha* means to be impetuous, or to behave violently and crazily. The word may have morphed from *gamusabori, musaboru* meaning to desire something deeply. *Musha* is written with the characters for warrior, but these characters are used purely for their phonetic value. So *gamushara* is a kind of eccentricity caused by the ravenous desires of *ga* (*Nihon kokugo daijiten* 1973, vol. 5). This means that although the *ga* should ordinarily be trained out of children as a negative trait, the self can be harnessed to positive effect.

The trained self is the one that carries out hard work. This is particularly beautifully expressed in the phrase 'with only his own feet to rely on' (*jibun no ashi dake ga tayori)*, used in story 93.1.2 to describe the father's work in setting up a business and building a home. The examples above show that hard work is also carried out for the sake of the self and one's own dreams and goals. It also seems from the use of the term *muga muchū* that the self that works (*jibun*) is different to the self that is selfish and obstinate (*ga* of *wagamama* and *gamushara*), and one works hard so that the former self can overcome the latter self. However, this hard work can sometimes be fuelled by a focus and drive that comes from the impetuous self (*gamusha*), which confirms the importance of personal desires as a positive motivating factor.

The use of words such as *yume* (dream) and *mokuhyō* (goal) also indicate the importance of ambition in the stories studied. The contents of these words are explained very clearly in story 93.1.3. In this story the father recalls his own motivation to work in his youth. To have a goal is 'such an important thing' (*donna ni taisetsu na mono*). His goal is described as a type of desire (*yoku*) that causes the father to practice playing baseball. One achievement 'links into the next goal' (*tsugi no mokuhyō ni tsunagaru*), which shows that a goal can prevent complacency.

He describes his dreams as 'to live with his grandfather in a big house', 'to have a beautiful wife', and, 'to have a beautiful car'. In story 93.1.5, to work in a zoo is described as a dream. In both of these cases the contents of dreams include moral behaviour such as caring for grandparents and working. Moral obligations are therefore integrated into the protagonists' personal dreams.

The argument I gave above for seeing moral instruction as enabling the development of self-reliance, rather than enforcing authoritarian moral codes, is essential in understanding the role of parental figures in moral education textbooks. While fathers do have the authority over the protagonists to tell them how to behave morally, this does not contradict the need for children to develop a sense of self. In fact, the role of the father is to inculcate self-consciousness as an individual to be successful in the wider world.

The Japanese work ethic is often described as powered by a sense of duty and putting the needs of the group above the individual (Hendry 1987: 137–8). However, in the idealised image of hard work given in textbooks for moral instruction, the protagonists' motivations are not based on the needs of the group. In fact, a wider group is never even mentioned, and the only sense of duty that appears in any story is man's responsibility towards domesticated animals, as portrayed in story 93.1.5. Hard work is in fact closely linked to a sense of selfhood and clear, individualised goals.

The Traveller who Did not Pass Twice – the Exception that Proves the Rule

Story 93.1.6 presents an unusual case in that the father figure does not hold any of the qualities described above. He is very talkative, discussing the rationale for almost all of his actions with his children. There is no mention of him having a job of any sort, let alone a job that takes him away from home. He also appears to have a close relationship with his son. They spend the entire story side by side, acting in tandem with each other. Most of their shared activities are moral errors, indicating that the father's close proximity and communication with his children is morally detrimental to all concerned.

In this story the family live in the mountains, in an area that becomes desolate out of the tourist season. On a stormy night a traveller calls on them asking for shelter. The father and son refuse to let the stranger into their home. The father does most of the talking, and the son gives short expressions of agreement and physical support in the form of a thick wooden pole that he grasps, ready to use against the stranger. Hearing the pained cries of his daughter, who is extremely unwell, the traveller gives rare medicine to the father and then leaves. The medicine cures the daughter from her illness, bringing her back from the brink of death. She grows into a beautiful woman and bears many children.

The father repeatedly doubts his own judgment. As soon as the traveller hands over the medicine the father begins to hesitate about his decision not to let the stranger into his home. When the medicine saves his daughters life, and later in life when he is playing with his grandchildren, he experiences condemnation from his conscience (*ryōshin ni semerareru*), indecision and regret about his actions. These are described as merciless (*nasakenaku*), poor treatment (*shiuchi*) and cold-hearted (*hakujō*). This is a direct contradiction to the example set by the other stories, in which the father's judgment is always correct.

This story might seem to contradict my thesis that the portrayal of fathers in moral education textbooks follows a uniform pattern that is morally instructive. However, I believe that this unusual story strengthens my argument. The father in this story is an example of the wrong father, who is not just talkative, jobless and too close to his son, but also makes a moral error so serious that he regrets it for his entire life. This demonstrates that silence and distance are portrayed as necessary qualities for a morally instructive father figure.

Furthermore, the precedent set by other stories, in which adult men who are not the father are portrayed as intimidating and unkind is turned on its head here, as the traveller is very polite, and turns out to be so kind as to save the life of the daughter. Not only does the father make a moral error in this story, but he is upstaged by the traveller, who is a model of kindness. However, towards the end of the story the people from the nearby village wonder whether this mysterious traveller might have been a *kami* (deity). This is the only case in my sample where an adult male who is not the father is portrayed as being kinder and more pleasant, and yet it turns out that he is no ordinary man. Therefore the position of the father as the kindest man in the protagonist's world is unchallenged. It is noteworthy in light of this that the father's desire to help his daughter is described as 'typical of a parent's compassion' (*sasuga oya no nasake*) – so that despite his errors and his merciless (*nasakenaku*) behaviour towards the traveller, the father's compassion is affirmed.

One theme from previous stories that holds in 93.1.6 is that of selfhood. This theme occurs in the last few paragraphs, when the whole family, particularly the father, are reflecting on their mistake. For example, 'Father regretted his own (*jibun no*) cold-heartedness,' or 'He thought that if a traveller ever comes to ask for something again, we ought to be as kind as we can be (*jibun ga dekiru dake*).' This confirms the centrality of selfhood in morally instructive stories.

CONCLUSIONS

In this dissertation I explained my analysis of stories from Japanese moral education textbooks against the historical and theoretical background of moral education and fatherhood in Japan. Based on these results, I made two arguments; first, I argued that moral education textbooks from both the 1960s and the 1990s taught a morality based on independent selfhood; secondly, I argued that the portrayal of fathers in accordance with the 'idealised past' view of fatherhood is closely connected to the teaching of a morality that emphasises focusing on one's own way and self-reliance.

My first argument concerns selfhood in moral education in Japan. The history of moral education in Japan has been a story of tension between the ideal of individual independence and the desire to inculcate harmonious social values in the state education system. While pre-war *shūshin* portrayed the self as an imperial subject in a greater national family, the 1947 Fundamental Law on Education stressed individualism, responsibility and independence. The re-establishment of moral education classes in post-occupation Japan was opposed by the JTU because of the view that weekly classes could not allow for the cultivation of individuality. Teachers' opposition has often been due to the idealisation of a close, personal teacher-student relationship; moral education classes are seen as too impersonal.

McVeigh sees moral education as an instrument of authority, designed to undermine people's ability to think for themselves and lock them into an authoritarian, statist structure. However, moral education and *shidō* are carried out as part of an intimate, egalitarian relationship and can encourage children to decide for themselves how to behave. In my analysis I found that moral education stories that feature a father teach a morality based on self-motivation and self-reliance. This contrasts with the arguments of both McVeigh and the JTU: moral education is not necessarily authoritarian, and weekly classes might not preclude the cultivation of individual ambitions.

In the post-war moral education stories in my sample, the home is a symbolic space that represents the *uchi*, the inner world and the inherently moral self. The home is the setting for the protagonist's re-discovery of him- or her-self, while outside of the home the protagonist takes steps towards transforming into a different kind of person who is better equipped to go out into society (*seken ni deru*).

This portrayal of the family as an inner circle from which the protagonist moves out into wider society mirrors long-standing trends in Japanese educational theory. In *kokoro no kyōiku* theories the family is portrayed as one of a series of widening circles that includes the state and the wider world. This may be seen as an echo of the pre-war vision of the nuclear family as part of a wider national family (*kokka*). In pre-war education, the self as an individual with personal desires was glossed over, and emphasis was placed on the self as a citizen of Japan and a subject of the Emperor. By contrast, in the post-war moral education textbooks I have analysed, a self-motivated individual is linked to the outside world by means of the *uchi/soto* division, not a link to a national figurehead. This indicates that even where *kokoro no kyōiku* theories appear to be played out in Japanese education, this does not necessarily lead to a subordination of the individual to nationalistic priorities.

In the stories I analysed, selfhood and hard work are portrayed as causally linked. A sense of self and personal dreams and goals are described as the main reason for working hard, while obligations to a wider group feature very little. This contradicts McVeigh's assertion (1998, 2004) that moral education in Japan locks people into an authoritarian structure. It also contrasts with LeTendre's findings (1999) concerning the importance of group harmony and responsibility in Japanese education; at least in the stories about the father, the pursuit of one's own aspirations is foremost promoted.

My second argument concerns the role of fictional fathers in this individualist moral education. In the stories I have analysed, fathers are consistently portrayed as men of few words who often work away from home. While they are physically distant and somewhat invisible (*mienai chichioya*), they are not emotionally distant and are in fact extraordinarily kind compared to other men. Their role is to carefully observe the child and transmit moral ideas in a way that is best suited to the child's individual situation.

One story stood out as an exceptional case of a talkative, morally fallible father, which proves the rule that the distance of fathers is essential to their role as moral guides. In the only case in which the father and son have a close relationship, behaving in tandem with one another and spending all of their time together, the father commits a moral error so serious that he regrets it for the rest of his life. This demonstrates that the ideal role of fathers in moral education textbooks is to quietly observe the protagonist from a distance, in order to teach them morality by guiding them towards the realisation and development of their moral self.

The fictional fathers in my sample encourage independence and self-motivation in the child by virtue of their distance and silence. However, this style of fathering is heavily criticised in Japan today. Dark, apocalyptic *anime* such as those analysed by Napier (2008) express a sense of isolation from fathers among young people in Japan. Sociologists such as Arai, Inuzaka and Hayashi (2005) have criticised the 'invisible father' and claimed that it damages the moral development of young people. Meanwhile, the government has started to encourage men to be more involved in their childrens' lives in order to boost the birthrate. There appears to be a dissonance between how people would like modern fathers to behave and how fathers are portrayed in moral education textbooks.

The stories I have analysed stretch across a historical period that includes the rise and decline of the social and economic conditions that supported the 'idealised past' image of the father. Even the more recently published stories in my sample show no change away from the portrayal of fathers as distant and silent. Yet by the time these more recent textbooks were published, the 'idealised past' of fatherhood was already becoming increasingly undesirable and even unfeasible given the economic changes Japan had undergone. The stories had not adapted to match these changes.

The loss of job security, as seen by the phenomenon of dramatically increasing freeters, means that the future ideal image of fathers who are more involved in their childrens' lives and less married to their jobs may be a necessity, as well as a dream. If this is the case, then stories such as those in my sample may change to reflect changing ideals. Such an adjustment will entail rewriting the relationship between fatherhood and selfhood in moral education textbooks. A fictional father who is not silent and absent will have to find new ways to teach the protagonist about self-discovery, the self in wider society, and self-motivated hard work.

APPENDIX: STORIES ANALYSED

(1966) *Atarashii seikatsu* (New lifestyle)

Junior high school year 1

66.1.1 'My name': Upon reflection on her parents' motives for choosing her name, the protagonist decides to use her name as a reminder to be a positive person.

66.1.2 'Sparrow': A boy is out walking in the garden with his father and dog when he sees a sparrow sacrificing her own life to save that of her children.

(1967) *Dōtoku no shidō shiryō* (Moral guidance materials)

Junior high school year 1

67.1.1 'Stubborn': A boy quarrels with his father. After a week of quiet sulking, the father goes away on business and leaves the son a letter. The son is uplifted by his father's actions, which he interprets as treating him as an equal.

67.1.2 'Father's regular letters': A rural family are separated from their father for years as he works in a distant prefecture. The father and his family regularly exchange letters and presents.

(1989) *Minna no dōtoku* (Everybody's morals)

Elementary school year 4

89.4.1 'Festival drums': A girl's father suggests that she try to play in the drum group for a festival. She practices very hard and the festival is a success. Her father praises her.

89.4.2 'One silver coin': A boy is given half of his father's earnings with which to buy groceries. On his way to the store he loses the money, and is upset. His mother finds him and gives him more money.

89.4.3 'U-turn': A family try to go camping, but halfway through their journey they find that the road is blocked. The father tells them they have to turn around and go home, and he points out that if you lose your life, you cannot get it back. The mother tells the children to listen to their father. The protagonist reflects that father had been thinking of their welfare.

89.4.4 'Mother quail': A boy goes hunting with his father and sees a quail sacrifice her life to protect her young. Father explains that the father quail will take over care of the young. They later return to the same area to find that this is the case.

89.4.5 'Had we been 30 minutes later': Father answers the door one evening to find paramedics there, asking for directions to a neighbour's house. The protagonist knows the way and directs them to the correct house. The following day, the father reads the newspaper out loud to his son, because the paramedics are quoted as saying that had they arrived 30 minutes later, the sick person would not have survived.

89.4.6 'A dangerous road': On a snowy day, a boy and his brother build a snowman. After an hour their father tells them to help him to clear the path of snow and they complain. Father explains that if the snow melts it will turn to ice overnight, and mother agrees with him. The next morning the parts of the path that were cleared are safer than the ones that were not. The boys help their school-teachers to clear a path to the classrooms.

(1993) *Ashita o hiraku* (opening tomorrow)

Junior high school year 1

93.1.1 'Extra salmon': A boy admits over Sunday dinner to having broken a neighbour's window. His mother offers to apologise on his behalf, but his father interjects and says that he must apologise himself for what he has done. The boy immediately runs out of the house and apologises, after much hesitation due to fear of the neighbour. When he returns home he finds the house empty as the family have gone fruit-picking, but his father has left him an extra piece of salmon to eat.

93.1.2 'Father's hands, mother's hands': After many years of dedicated hard work, a girl's father is incapacitated by illness and her mother works harder to compensate. Eventually he recovers and the girl decides that she wants to work hard as well.

93.1.3 'From father to you': A father tells the story of when he was a young man and he learned to cease his roguish ways and trained hard to become a successful baseball player.

93.1.4 'One postcard': A boy goes on a hiking trip with his friends to see his uncle. His uncle is extraordinarily kind and hospitable to them. Weeks after their return, the boy's father receives a postcard from the uncle, who politely points out that the boy never sent a thank you note. The boy's father reads him the postcard and he regrets his inaction.

93.1.5 'One phrase from my father': A young man facing a crisis in his career as a zookeeper returns to his hometown to take a break from the pressures of his job. His father tells him 'Your otters are lonely', which the man instantly understands to be a message about man's responsibility to animals. He hurriedly returns to the zoo and embraces his otters.

93.1.6 'The traveller that did not pass twice': A family living on an isolated mountain are tending to their sick daughter in a storm. A traveller comes knocking on the door asking for shelter. The father answers the door and refuses to let the traveller in. Hearing the pained cries of the daughter, the traveller gives the father medicine and then disappears. The medicine saves the daughter's life, and the father regrets his actions forever.

(1996) *Ashita o hiraku* (Opening tomorrow)

Junior high school, year 1

96.1.1 'Pencils in a wooden box': After studying abroad, a young man returns home to begin his career as a writer. He gets very few commissions, and in his despair asks his father, a composer, if he was always talented. The father explains that he believed that he was always talented because he was chosen for the school band as a child, but later learned that he was chosen not for his musical talent but his lung capacity. He shows his son three wooden boxes under the piano that are filled with pencils worn down until they were no longer useable, and tells him that if he has no natural ability he should create it.

REFERENCES

Adams, Don (1960). 'Rebirth of Moral Education in Japan,' *Comparative Education Review* 4/1, pp. 61–64.

Adams, Don and Oshiba Mamoru (1961). 'Japanese Education: After the Americans Left', *Peabody Journal of Education* 39/1, pp. 9–19.

Arai Ikuo, Inuzaka Fumio and Hayashi Yasunari (2005). *Dōtoku kyōiku ron* (Essays on moral education). Tōkyō: NHK Books.

Cave, Peter (2004). '"Bukatsudō": The Educational Role of Japanese School Clubs,' *Journal of Japanese Studies* 30/2, pp. 383–415.

Cummings, William (2003). 'Why Reform Japanese Education?', Roger Goodman and David Phillips (eds) *Can the Japanese Change Their Education System?* Oxford: Symposium Books, pp. 31–42.

Dasgupta, Romit (2003). 'Creating Corporate Warriors: the Salaryman and Masculinity in Japan', Kam Louie and Morris Low (eds) *Asian Masculinities*. New York: Routledge, pp. 118–133.

Duke, Benjamin (1964). 'The New Guide for Teaching Moral Education in Japan', *Comparative Education Review* 8/2, pp. 186–190.

Egawa Binsei et al. [Takahashi Masaru, Hayo Masaaki, Mochizuki Shigenobu] (2003). *Saishin kyōiku kiiwādo 137* (The latest educational keywords 137). Tōkyō: Jiji News Agency.

Fukuzawa Yukichi (1960). *The Autobiography of Fukuzawa Yukichi* [1899]. Tōkyō: Hokuseido Press.

Gordon, Andrew (2003). *A Modern History of Japan. From Tokugawa Times to the Present.* Oxford: Oxford University Press.

Hendry, Joy (1987). *Understanding Japanese Society.* Oxford: Oxford University Press.

Higashi, Julie (2008). 'The *kokoro* Education: Landscaping the Minds and Hearts of Japanese,' David Grossman and Joe Tin-Yau Lo (eds) *Social Education in Asia: Critical Issues and Multiple Perspectives.* Charlotta, Ca: Information Age

Publishing, pp. 39–56.

Honda Yuki (2005). '"Freeters": Young Atypical Workers in Japan', *Japan Labour Review* 2/3, pp. 5–25.

Horio Teruhisa, Namimoto Katsutoshi and Ishiyama Hisao (2003). *Ima, naze kaeru? Kyōiku kihonhō Q&A* (Why change it now? Fundamental Law of Education Q&A). Tōkyō: Otsuki Shoten.

Khan Yoshimitsu (1997). *Japanese Moral Education Past and Present*. Plainsboro: Associated University Presses.

Lanham, Betty (1979). 'Ethics and Moral Principles Taught in Schools of Japan and the United States,' *Ethos* 7/1, pp. 1–18.

LeTendre, Gerald (1994). 'Guiding Them on: Teaching, Hierarchy and Social Organisation in Japanese Middle Schools', *Journal of Japanese Studies* 20/1, pp. 37–59.

LeTendre, Gerald (1999). 'Community-building Activities in Japanese Schools: Alternative Paradigms of the Democratic School,' *Comparative Education Review* 43/3, pp. 283–310.

Luhmer, Klaus (1990). 'Moral Education in Japan', *Journal of Moral Education* 19/3, pp. 172–182.

Marshall, Byron (1994). *Learning to be Modern: Japanese Political Discourse on Education*. Oxford: Westview Press.

Mathews, Gordon (2003). 'Can a "Real Man" Live for his Family? Ikigai and Masculinity in Today's Japan', James Roberson and Suzuki Nobue (eds) *Men and Masculinities in Contemporary Japan. Dislocating the Salaryman Doxa*. London: RoutledgeCurzon, pp. 109–124.

McVeigh, Brian (1998). 'Linking State and Self: How the Japanese State Bureaucratises Subjectivity through Moral Education', *Anthropological Quarterly* 71/3, pp. 125–137.

McVeigh, Brian (2004). *Nationalisms of Japan*. Totowa: Rowman and Littlefield.

Mori Arinori (2009). *Life and Resources in America*. Charleston: BiblioLife.

Napier, Susan (2008). 'From Spiritual Fathers to Tokyo Godfathers: Depictions of the Family in Japanese Animation', John Traphagan and Hashimoto Akiko (eds) *Imagined*

Families, Lived Families: Culture and Kinship in Contemporary Japan. Albany, NY: SUNY Press, pp. 33–50.

Nihon Daijiten Kankōkai (1973). *Nihon kokugo daijiten* (Japan national language dictionary) Vol. 5. Tōkyō: Shōgakkan.

Nihon Shakaika Kyōiku Gakkai (Japan Social Studies Education Research Association) (2000). *Shakaika kyōiku jiten* (An encyclopedia of social studies education). Tōkyō: Gyōsei.

Oshiba Mamoru (1961). 'Moral Education in Japan', *The School Review* 69/2, pp. 227–244.

Roberson, James and Suzuki Nobue (2003). 'Introduction', James Roberson and Suzuki Nobue (eds) *Men and Masculinities in Contemporary Japan: Dislocating the Salaryman Doxa*, Richmond, Surrey: RoutledgeCurzon, pp. 1–19.

Roberts, Glenda (2002). 'Pinning Hopes on Angels. Reflections from an Ageing Japan's Urban Landscape', Roger Goodman (ed.) *Family and Social Policy in Japan.* Cambridge: Cambridge University Press, pp. 54–91.

Rose, Caroline (2006). 'Patriotic Education in Japan', Shimazu Naoko (ed.) *Nationalisms in Japan.* London: Routledge.

Shimbori Michiya (1960). 'A Historical and Social Note on Moral Education in Japan', *Comparative Education Review* 4/2, pp. 97–101.

Smiles, Samuel (1869). *Self Help. With Illustrations of Character and Conduct.* New York: Harper.

Spradley, James (1979). *The Ethnographic Interview.* Fort Worth et al.: Harcourt Brace Jvanovic College Publishers.

Swale, Alistair (2000). *The Political Thought of Mori Arinori. A Study in Meiji Conservatism.* London: Routledge.

Toyama-Bialke, Chisaki (2003) 'The Japanese Triangle', Gesine Foljanty-Jost (ed.) *Juvenile Delinquency in Japan. Reconsidering the 'Crisis'.* Leiden: Brill, pp. 19–50.

Traphagan, John and Hashimoto Akiko (2008). 'Changing Japanese Families', John Traphagan and Hashimoto Akiko (eds) *Imagined Families, Lived Families*, op. cit., pp. 1–12.

4 All the World's a Stage

Herbivore Boys and the Performance of Masculinity in Contemporary Japan

Chris Deacon

Supervisors: Mark Morris and Brigitte Steger (2012)

Table of Contents

I wish to thank Dr Brigitte Steger for her assistance and enthusiasm during the research and writing of this dissertation and Dr Mark Morris for his continued support throughout my undergraduate degree.

Names of the interviewees are pseudonyms.

INTRODUCTION

'*Otoko wa dame ni natta!*' ('men have become useless!') – this is the cry from many *oyaji*, or older men, concerning young Japanese males in the twenty-first century (Fukasawa 2009: 3). The discourse surrounding these 'useless' men in the media has posed that a new breed of young males called *sōshokukei danshi* (herbivorous boys or men) are changing Japanese society. These young men are said to lead selfish lifestyles rather than living for the sake of a company or family. They are rarely seen in a positive light, and many have referred to their emergence as a crisis in Japanese masculinity (see *Telegraph* 2011; NPR 2009; *Japan Times* 2009a; *Nihon Keizai Shimbun* 2010 etc). English academic literature on *sōshokukei danshi*, at the time of writing, is limited to a brief mention in one book on Japanese youth (see Toivonen and Imoto 2012: 2), and while Japanese literature on 'herbivores' does exist, academic research is yet to be carried out.

In this dissertation, I go beyond media discourse to explore what is really happening to young Japanese men. My primary source material includes semi-structured interviews with thirty-five male undergraduates – some of whom identified as *sōshokukei* and some of whom did not – which I conducted in Kyoto in Spring 2011 and Winter 2012. These interviews compliment media sources and wider secondary literature in gaining an accurate image of the lifestyles and attitudes of young Japanese men in contemporary society.

Having outlined the discourse surrounding *sōshokukei danshi* and the ideas of these men themselves, I analyse masculinity in Japanese society more broadly. To fully understand the changes which are occurring in masculine practice, it is necessary to establish the dominant patterns of masculinity up to this point. I outline these dominant masculinities in recent history and contemporary Japan, and explore the lifestyles of the men who subscribe to hegemonic gender ideology.

Using gender theory, in particular, theories of 'performance', I then go on to explore how Japanese males become gendered. I do this by analysing both school education and the home environment to discover what gender lessons Japanese children learn. With this theory of performance in mind, I then establish how hegemonic masculinity in Japanese society might be subverted. I suggest that this process is already occurring with the increase in so-called 'freeters' (*furiitā*, i.e. workers lacking full-time employment contracts), the growing popularity of beautified males and the decline of marriage.

Finally, I relate wider subversion of hegemonic masculinity by young Japanese males to *sōshokukei danshi*, suggesting that the two phenomena overlap to a great extent and explore how these males are rebelling against hegemonic gender ideology. I argue that these young men are not just one isolated grouping, but instead represent a wider shift towards multiple gender ideologies becoming permissible in Japanese society.

GRASS-EATING MEN

The Discourse on Herbivores

In December 2011, the Japanese magazine *SPA!* published an article about the new 'PlayStation Vita'. The headline read '*Gaiken wa sōshokukei demo kinō wa nikushokukei*' ('It looks herbivorous, but its features are carnivorous') (*SPA!* 2011). During the five years preceding this article, the phrase '*sōshoku*' (grass-eater) or '*sōshokukei*' (literally, 'grass-eating type') had gained currency in Japanese society to the extent that readers of this magazine had no trouble in understanding the meaning of the headline. In its original usage, however, the term describes society's perception of the seemingly changing lifestyle of young men in contemporary Japan.

The phrase *sōshoku danshi* was first coined by Fukasawa Maki,[5] a freelance writer and marketing expert, in an article on the *Nikkei Business* website in October 2006. Fukasawa used the phrase to describe young men who are heterosexual but are not assertive (*sekkyokuteki*) in trying to pursue women (*Nikkei Business* 2006). At that time, the phrase was not picked up by the media and did not receive much attention. However, in April 2008 the popular women's magazine *Non-no* ran a special report on *sōshoku danshi*, stating that a revolution in men's attitudes to love was taking place. Women were told they would have to become more assertive to make up for the new men. This article was very influential and by 2009 several books had been published, their contents ranging from self-diagnosis of being herbivorous to strategies for herbivorous men in the workplace (see Ichibanchō 2009; Okuda 2009). That year, *sōshokukei* became a media buzzword and was ranked in the top ten 'keywords of the year'. The phrase was also picked up abroad, with several media organisations, especially in the United

---

[5] Fukasawa wrote of *sōshoku* men, without using *kei*. However, in the years since, *sōshokukei* has come to be the most common terminology. The difference in meaning is minimal, with the *kei* suggesting a certain type or kind of male.

States and United Kingdom, running stories on the issue (Lifestudies.org).

The discourse on *sōshokukei danshi* has varied over time (Morioka 2011: 13). While, at first, it only concerned young men's attitudes to love, relationships and sex, it quickly came to encompass entire lifestyles. Commentators discussed working life, appearance, values and relationships. Ushikubo Megumi, a marketing researcher, has summarised the characteristics of *sōshokukei danshi* as being uncompetitively minded about jobs; being fashion conscious, enjoying shopping; being uninterested in dating, relationships or sex, and being thrifty with money (*Japan Times* 2009a). Figure 1 shows some of the characteristics put forward by the *Yomiuri Shimbun* which represent the likes and dislikes of a generalised *sōshokukei danshi*, accompanied by my English translation.

The image of 'herbivore boys'

* Prefers his favourite drink over 'downing a beer'
* Slim and doesn't eat much
* Loves desserts and sweets
* Fashion-conscious
* Enthusiastic about ecology
* Good relationship with parents
* Inseparable from his mobile
* Even splits the bill for [love] hotels

Fig. 1: The image of 'herbivore boys' (*Yomiuri Online* 2009).

The books written on *sōshokukei danshi* have, however, been fairly consistent in their appraisal of these males' attitudes to sex and relationships. They are said to generally dislike sex or even having a girlfriend (Ushikubo 2008: 58). Whereas older generations of men are '*gatsu gatsu*' (greedy) in their pursuit of sex, *sōshokukei danshi* are said to be the complete opposite (Takeuchi 2010: 13–14). That is to say, they are much more passive (*shōkyokuteki*) in their attitude to relationships and asking women on dates (*kokuru*) (Fukasawa 2009: 104). Given the significant domestic and international media attention afforded to Japan's declining birthrate and aging society (*shōshi-kōrei-ka*), it is unsurprising that this feature of *sōshokukei danshi* has been emphasised most. Moral panic in both the Japanese and foreign media regarding what men might be 'turning into' has included statistics stating that as many as a third of young Japanese men are 'uninterested in sex', with 'experts' stating that the only factor that needs to be looked at in this problem is that 'young men are not having sex' (*Telegraph* 2009).

Such blurring of Japan's societal problems with the *sōshokukei danshi* phenomenon has been strong (Takeuchi 2010: 81). For example, newspaper articles have blamed 'herbivore men shunning sex' for the declining birthrate (see Reuters 2009). This has also extended to the issue of plummeting marriage rates, with fathers complaining that their herbivore sons 'maybe are not capable of marriage' (*kekkon dekinai kamo*) (*Nihon Keizai Shimbun* 2010). Moreover, the media regularly claim *sōshokukei danshi* are impacting the Japanese economy negatively as they prefer temporary or non-regular work over the salaryman style of regular white-collar employment, and are thrifty with their money, having no interest in extravagant purchases (see *Yomiuri Online* 2009).

Surveys asking young Japanese men whether or not they classify themselves as *sōshokukei* have consistently shown that

between 50 and 70 percent do so.[6] Such a large proportion identifying as *sōshokukei* means that this issue simply cannot be ignored.

Work, Fashion and Love

Media organisations are, of course, likely to focus on the most
sensational aspects of issues. The issue of *sōshokukei danshi* has
been no exception, with foreign media often relating it to an
obsession with the cyber world and anime and manga characters
(see *Guardian* 2011). However, from analysing primary source
material, especially talking to young men who identify as
sōshokukei, it might be possible to get a clearer idea of this
phenomenon and offer some explanation for the statistics
mentioned in the media which, though framed in a sensationalist
context, are valid (see IPSS 2011). I will look at three issues in
particular which are relevant to *sōshokukei danshi*: working habits,
shopping/fashion and relationships.

    Sōshokukei danshi are said to be uninterested in careers,
especially in the corporate world (*Clarín* 2009). Self-diagnosis
books published for potential herbivores include statements such as
'I have dreams', 'I don't want a job with lots of overtime', 'I don't
want to have to drink alcohol with colleagues after work' and 'I
don't want to be a salaryman' (Ushikubo 2009: 46, 50). Personal
accounts of self-identified *sōshokukei danshi* support this idea.
Talking with Morioka Masahiro, interviewee Ninakawa-san spoke
about following his childhood ambition to become a professional
cake maker. He started baking cakes as a hobby in high school and,
although friends were surprised at first, they enjoyed his cakes
greatly and eventually got used to it. Hearing positive reviews of

---

[6] See *Nihon Keizai Shimbun* 2010; Ushikubo 2008: 38; NPR 2009; *Japan Times*
2009a; *Yomiuri Online* 2009 etc for a variety of surveys, carried out by
organisations such as Unilever, which all produced a similarly high figure. In
Japan, many suggested to me that even the Japanese government had surveyed
men on this issue, however I was unable to find evidence of this.

his creations gives him great satisfaction that he would not find working for a big company. He cares more about enhancing his personal skills than concentrating on climbing up a company hierarchy (Morioka 2009: 94–96).

My own interviews with male university students in Kyoto followed this pattern. Those who identified as *sōshokukei* were generally against entering the corporate world. For example, Matsumoto-kun was quite clear that, while he was not sure what he *did* want to do, he definitely did not want to be a salaryman. He did not want to live and work for the sake of a company (*'kaisha no tame ni'*) and found corporate culture and the life of a salaryman abhorrent (*'zettai iya da!'*). Sugiyama-kun, on the other hand, was quite sure about what he wanted to do. Currently studying foreign languages, he had decided to become a translator and maybe live abroad. However, he did not want to be tied down to a particular company and described his dream lifestyle as a freelance worker.

This dislike of company life is also clear in another self-diagnosis book. Thirty *sōshokukei danshi* who had been inter-viewed in the course of researching the book are listed, along with their professions. Of all thirty, only two are listed as *kaisha'in* (company employees), with the rest having an assortment of jobs including hairdresser, yoga instructor, café waiter and clothing shop assistant (Ichibanchō 2009: 111). This is in stark contrast to 'traditional' career expectations for Japanese men, which I explore in the next chapter. The pattern seems to be that *sōshokukei danshi* are far more confident in asserting their own individual dreams and aspirations, rather than believing they have any kind of duty to stick to rigid gender norms which would see them working for a large company.

An association also exists between *sōshokukei danshi* and shopping, in particular for fashion and cosmetic items. While these men are supposedly thrifty with their money and dislike making expensive purchases, they are also very aesthetically conscious (Ushikubo 2008: 4). The media has reported on this aspect too, often writing about young herbivore men receiving 'traditionally female' beauty treatments, such as eyebrow plucking and facials (see NPR 2009). They are said to never be without their facial blotting paper (*aburatori-gami*), which has become increasingly popular in recent years (Ichibanchō 2009: 57). Some companies, such as Shiseido, have even begun to specifically target *sōshokukei danshi* and have launched special men's versions of beauty products. One Shiseido employee summarised the change in attitude by saying 'men's obsessions have shifted from automobiles to their own appearance' (*Japan Times* 2009b).

Dōshisha University, where I studied from September 2010 to August 2011, was seemingly full of such aesthetically conscious young men. Even those who considered themselves *kōha* (literally 'hard') often had dyed or permed hair and made sure their clothes were of the latest fashion.[7] Those self-identifying as *sōshokukei danshi* were very fashion-conscious and often spoke of it being '*taisetsu*' (important, valuable) to them. Takeda-kun stated that his fashion sense allowed him to be himself ('*boku wa boku*'), choosing what *he* liked and enjoyed wearing. Use of cosmetics was also very popular, with many having dyed hair and/or wearing make-up. This was not seen as strange or unusual, but rather it was '*atarimae*' (obvious) that one should want to look one's best. This desire to make oneself as aesthetically pleasing as possible was very common in *sōshokukei danshi* I interviewed.

The final issue I will look at is the romantic relationships of *sōshokukei danshi*. Much has been made in the media of the apparent disinterest of herbivore men in finding a girlfriend or having sex. The foreign media have sometimes suggested that these men may be entirely asexual (see *Huffington Post* 2011). The bulk of literature in Japan, however, takes a very different view and does pose these men as wanting romantic relationships, but in a different style to older generations. Morioka Masahiro's two books on

---

[7] One particular trend for men during my time at Dōshisha was wearing patterned leggings beneath shorts. This was *incredibly* popular, with droves of male students showing off this style.

sōshokukei danshi deal with advice on love and relationships; one for herbivores themselves and another for females who would like a herbivore boyfriend (Morioka 2008, Morioka 2009). His understanding is that most *sōshokukei danshi* would not mind having a girlfriend, and maybe even eventually marrying, but for now would rather concentrate on themselves (*jibun o taisetsu ni suru*), their own pursuits, interests and ambitions, rather than worrying about having to please a girlfriend (Morioka 2009: 17). This could explain the common complaint in the media that *sōshokukei danshi* are passive, rather than assertive, with women.

Perhaps due to the personal nature of this topic, it was difficult to elicit lengthy responses from the students I interviewed. The majority of *sōshokukei danshi* did not have girlfriends – a common response was '*shō ga nai nā*' ('what can you do?'). Some suggested that they probably could have a girlfriend if they were to try harder, but they did not have the *yaruki* (will power) to do so. When asked if he had a girlfriend, Kawamura-kun simply said '*kanojo ga inakute mo betsu ni ii*' ('I haven't got a girlfriend, but that's fine'). This feeling of ambivalence to the idea of finding a girlfriend was very common, with none of my *sōshokukei* interviewees suggesting they were keen on having a relationship soon. It is difficult to know for sure whether these answers were entirely honest, or whether the shyness of my interviewees had an influence on these answers. While most discourse on *sōshokukei danshi* suggests that they do not particularly enjoy or seek out sexual relationships, Figure 1 suggests they may use love hotels. This shows that there are diverse views on whether or not *sōshokukei danshi* go on dates and are sexually active. Fukasawa suggests that they often *literally* 'sleep with' girls in a love hotel after going out at night, without it being at all sexual (*Nikkei Business* 2006).

Chris Deacon

Post-bubble Boys

The image of *sōshokukei danshi* from the sources I have outlined in this chapter seems to have a clear pattern running through it: the importance of the self. These men do not want to be one of the many corporate warriors of a large company; they want to follow their own dreams and ambitions, doing a job that gives them satisfaction. They do not want to be aesthetically unattractive; they want to be fashionable and to beautify themselves with cosmetics so that they can look their best. They do not want to have to worry about finding a girlfriend or maintaining a relationship; they want to concentrate on themselves and their own lives without extra responsibilities. In short, it seems that these men want to be individuals, who do what they want to do.

Why might this be the case? Literature on *sōshokukei danshi* often suggests that one cause may be the fathers of these men – a rebellion against their fathers' lifestyles. These fathers, who had their best years during Japan's bubble economy, were defined by their loyalty to and hard work for their company and the Japanese economy, with very little time for themselves or at home with their families (Fukasawa 2009: 104). This was the dominant ideology for adult males and to a large extent still is for their generation. The *sōshokukei danshi*, however, have never known the 'good times' of the bubble economy and were raised in a generation of economic decline (Ushikubo 2008: 21). With seemingly nothing to gain from working hard (*ganbaru*) for a large company, *sōshokukei danshi* are, instead, rejecting the salaryman generation of their fathers and asserting their individuality (NPR 2009). Along these lines, in an interview for *Bloomberg*, self-described herbivore Daisuke-kun complains that while his father's generation was rewarded for their hard work, he knows his generation will not be and therefore does not see the point of attempting a lifestyle similar to his father's (*Bloomberg* 2009).

Conclusion

The discourse regarding *sōshokukei danshi* is framed in notions of gender roles and expectations regarding the kind of lifestyle men 'should' be leading. Media and popular discourse has suggested that these young males prefer non-regular or part-time work; they regularly use beauty aesthetic treatments and products; and they are passive towards women, without desiring romantic relationships. My own interviewees have supported these ideas, with many *sōshokukei danshi* stressing the importance of being true to themselves. This attitude has resulted in a rejection of the 'salary-man lifestyle', which places far more emphasis on dedicating oneself to a company, with little time to focus on the self. The lifestyle and values of *sōshokukei danshi* are, therefore, a strong departure from 'traditional' expectations of male behaviour in post-war Japan. In order to contextualise this discussion, it is necessary to explore these traditional expectations and analyse wider notions of masculinity in Japanese society in the recent past and the present.

HEGEMONIC MASCULINITY

The Concept of Hegemonic Masculinity

While the visibility and frequency of non-dominant gender practices in Japanese society has increased markedly, in order to fully appreciate the shifts occurring in gender ideology and practice, we also need to examine the dynamics that operate *within* dominant discourses on gender (Dasgupta 2005: 168). That is to say, before we get to grips with what may be behind recent shifts in masculine practice, such as the emergence of *sōshokukei danshi*, we must first understand what these men are shifting from.

Sociologist R. W. Connell argues that although various masculinities exist in all societies and throughout history, often a dominant form exists which is referred to as 'hegemonic masculinity'.[8] Such hegemonic masculinity can be defined as the configuration of gender practice which best legitimates patriarchy and dominance of males in society. This idea pervades the lives of all males, whether they want it to or not. For example, in a school, sporting prowess might define a boy's masculinity, whether he enjoys or hates sport. Of course, it would be highly unlikely for every boy to be a skilled sportsman. Indeed, it is probably only the minority who posses such skills. Thus, in no way does hegemonic masculinity equate to the norm or average of males (Connell 2005: 77, 37). However, it is possible to still support this hegemony, for example by cheering the school sports team without actually competing. In this way, many males who do not practise such masculinity themselves are complicit in its hegemony. When there is a rebellion against this fixed idea of manliness, an attempt at

---

[8] Note the use of the plural form 'masculinities'. Connell (2005) stresses that this is the correct way to understand the practices of men: they are plural and diverse rather than singular and homogenous. Due to linguistic feel, the singular form 'masculinity' is sometimes preferable, though the above should be borne in mind.

correction often ensues from bystanders. Boys who do not achieve legitimacy at school, for example, may be taunted with words associated with femininity or homosexuality, such as 'sissy' or 'fag' (Connell 2005: 79).

This concept of hegemonic masculinity can be observed in Japanese society past and present. Connell (2005: 204) herself has referred to Japan as 'the most impenetrable patriarchy among the major powers'. Based on a study of male university students, Itō Kimio (1996) has argued that there is a 'fixation' (*kodawari*) with manliness in Japanese society.[9] The responses of his interviewees fell into two categories. One stated with confidence that they were manly (*boku wa otoko-rashii desu*), offering reasons such as physical strength and lusting after girls. The other stated that they were not manly (*otoko-rashikunai*) because they lacked the above traits. Thus, all defined their own masculinity by a hegemonic practice (of physical strength, sexual appetite for women etc), whether or not they actually possessed these characteristics. The latter group still subscribed to the orthodox view of what it means 'to be a man', despite believing they did not fit such a mold. None sought to challenge this hegemony with alternative ideas of masculinity (Itō 1996: 23, 24).

Hegemonic Masculinities in Japanese History

Such ideas of manliness are by no means recent phenomena. For example, dominant masculine ideologies can be seen in Japan's Warring States period in the form of *samurai*, who have been seen by many to represent the ideal Japanese male (Mason 2011: 74). That is not to say, however, that they were necessarily glorified as

---

[9] Generally Japanese texts on the topic use the word *otoko-rashisa* which is far closer to 'manliness' than 'masculinity'. One might argue that *otoko-rashisa* is similar to the concept of hegemonic masculinity as it is related to a dominant expectation of 'manliness'. However, some Japanese writers do speak of the possibility of multiple *otoko-rashisa*, such as Fukasawa (2009).

such at the time of their existence. Rather, it is necessary to look to the Meiji period for such discourse. Nitobe Inazō's *Bushidō: The Soul of Japan* (1905) celebrates the martial spirit of the hardy warriors of the Warring States period as the epitome of manliness. The Tokugawa shogunate used the concept of *bushidō* for this purpose, as did Meiji, Taishō and early Shōwa administrations, in the effort to militarise Japan (Low 2003: 86).

Thus, the self-sacrificing soldier became the epitome of manliness during Japan's militarisation. Ideas of a militaristic manliness were disseminated in schools and military training, ultimately leading to a Japanese military culture which socialised soldiers into merciless aggressors. Records from the Allied Translator and Interpreter Service state that notions associated with *bushidō*, such as battle cries and kendo, were used to socialise boys into military culture. Such physicality acted as a bodily practice which reinforced links to samurai ideals of masculinity (Low 2003: 83, 86). The 'comfort women' (*ianfu*) issue can also be seen as a clear example of a brutal hegemonic masculinity being exercised during the war period. Brothels and the battlefield were both locations for the production of gender, and the involvement of the Japanese government in the former illustrates the close relationship between the construction of masculinity in Japan and the needs of the state (Low 2003: 91). In this way, Japan's aggressive military man can be seen as the dominant masculinity of the time. With links to *bushidō* strongly stressed, the government and military used this gender identity to its advantage in its aggressive expansion into Asia.

Rise of the Salaryman

The end of the war saw an emasculation of Japan's military forces as symbolised by the meeting between Emperor Hirohito and General MacArthur, with the latter towering over the former in height and stature (Low 2003: 93). In defeat, therefore, Japanese men were also in danger of emasculation since they no longer had a militaristic motherland to fight for. These men were transformed into salarymen and factory workers, who now worked for the nation in a different context (Low 2003: 96). However, the militaristic (*gunjiteki*) link to masculinity continued in the realm of business (Taga 2006: 100). The object of the warriors' devotion and the tools of their trade changed, with battles now fought in the office, not in the field. Loyalty was now due to the company, rather than to their clan or the Emperor. However, they remained true to the 'samurai spirit', with their masculine ideals staying strong (Frühstück 2007: 56).

A salaryman (*sarariiman*) is a white-collar, male employee of a private sector organisation, typically characterised by such features as lifetime employment, seniority-based salaries and promotions, and a paternalistic concern for the employee on the part of the company in return for steady and diligent loyalty. Values associated with *bushidō*, such as duty, loyalty, self-sacrifice and endurance, which were previously used to glorify the soldier, are also ascribed to the salaryman (Dasgupta 2003: 119, 120). For example, there are many commonplace militaristic expressions used in businesses such as *kigyō senshi* (corporate warrior), *messhi hōkō* (selfless devotion) and *ichiba senryaku* (marketplace tactics/ strategy) (Taga 2006: 100). With the end of the war, the salaryman became the new Japanese male – the embodiment of a modern, industrialised and urban Japan (Dasgupta 2003: 121).

The hegemonic nature of salaryman masculinity leads to there being a highly prescribed way that salarymen must act. Several guides, one of which I explore in the next chapter, have been published on how salarymen should behave (Dasgupta 2003: 124). These requirements are not only limited to the workplace – a man's profession and his overall life (in the home and everywhere else) are inexorably linked. His transition from student to *shakaijin* (adult member of society) does not take place at the coming-of-age ceremony in the January of his twentieth year, but rather on his first day in a full-time job (McLelland 2005: 98). When he has such a job, he is capable of providing for himself and his future wife and children.

This hegemonic ideal, placing the man as a husband, father and, most importantly, provider to his family is embodied in the term *daikokubashira*, literally meaning the central supporting pillar of a house (Dasgupta 2005: 168). Marriage, in the highly hetero-normative society of Japan, has been close to compulsory for these men. Hidaka Tomoko has stated that it can be condensed into the words *atarimae* and *jōshiki* (obvious, common sense) (Hidaka 2010: 83). Being unmarried carries the implication of not being *ichininmae* (a fully independent member of society), but rather *hanninmae*, someone who is 'half a person' – not an independent adult but a child still waiting to grow up (Lunsing 2001: 75). To not marry is, thus, seen as non-compliance or even an active rejection of the responsibilities of being a good citizen (Dasgupta 2005: 173). It is even sometimes punished in the workplace. Informants regularly claim that unmarried men are passed over for promotion and can rarely reach higher than *kachō* (section head) in their company (Murata 2000: 541). Conversely, for a husband the same necessity is attached to finding a full-time job, preferably in salaryman-style 'regular' employment. As anthropologist Anne Allison puts it, a husband who does not work has 'no meaning' in Japan (Allison 1994: 91). One thirty year old salaryman inter-viewed by Romit Dasgupta stated: 'Not having a job is frightening – like being an animal that can't hunt its food' (Dasgupta 2005: 171). Thus, hegemonic masculinity strongly ties work and marriage together in Japanese society.

Indeed, hegemonic masculinity can be seen to affect the very meaning of Japanese men's lives. A common Japanese word used for this topic is *ikigai*, which is similar to the French *raison d'être* or 'reason to live'. Asking what it means 'to be a man' can often simply lead to jokes or embarrassed comments, and so asking about *ikigai*, instead, is a less direct, and therefore more efficient, route to understanding these issues. In his research on this subject, Gordon Mathews found that the majority of men place work as their *ikigai*

(Mathews 2003: 110). In some cases, *ikigai* was with the family, however this was problematic due to the continuing adherence of men to rigid gender roles in Japanese society. Those who did claim family as *ikigai* seemed to only do so on the basis that they were 'breadwinners' and thus could be seen to be indirectly choosing work as their *ikigai* (Mathews 2003: 114). The pressure felt by men to have work as their *ikigai* is immense. One interviewee stated that he hated his work but his family simply could not be his *ikigai* as he would be considered *memeshii* (effeminate) if that were the case. He even stated that he was jealous of women being able to lead this life (Mathews 2003: 117). Much of this pressure also comes from the Japanese state and economic order. Workers, such as these salarymen, are molded to believe that their sacrifice of themselves to their companies (with long hours etc) represents their 'apotheosis as men' rather than exploitation (Mathews 2003: 111).

Hegemonic masculinity can also be observed in the media. Analysing these media is relevant because they can create, reflect and reinforce dominant gender ideologies (Roberson 2005: 366). For example, in the advertising of Japanese *genki* drinks (energy drinks), images of hegemonic masculinity are seldom missing. One brand, Liptovan-D, uses the masculine plain form of the copula in its newspaper advertising: '*Sō da. Faito da. Liptovan-D da.*' (literally 'That's right. It's a fight. It's Liptovan-D.'), implying a manly edge. This is extended to a gruff, deep male voiceover in its television advertising (Roberson 2005: 369). Some advertising even places the hegemonic stereotype on men who famously do not abide by it, for example the golfer Maruyama Shigeki, who advertises Alinamin-V as a white-collar salaryman. Maruyama emerges from his house looking tired, at which point his wife gives him the drink and he is suddenly revitalised and jets off into the sky (Roberson 2005: 370). The breadwinning salaryman, tired from work but still dedicated to his job, supported by his stay-at-home wife – this has been Japan's post-war hegemonic masculinity.

Conclusion

The salaryman represents hegemonic masculine ideology in Japanese society, illustrating the highly gendered nature of this society and the importance of ties between working habits and gender. With apparent origins in *bushidō* still glorified, a path from samurai to soldier to salaryman can be traced. Whether samurai ever adhered to the *bushidō* ideal or not is largely irrelevant; the point is that the discourse on *bushidō*'s influence on the salaryman ideology has been compelling and wide-ranging. All three of these hegemonic masculinities in Japan's history have emphasised fighting for the nation. However, this has progressed from physical war in battlefields to economic war in offices and boardrooms. But how is it that Japanese males come to subscribe to this masculinity? To fully inform this discussion, it is necessary to analyse how Japanese males become gendered.

PERFORMING MASCULINITY

Learning to be Gendered

Although often blurred in popular discourse, gender is not something with which humans are innately born; it is not biological sex distinction. Rather, it is a social construct which applies specific roles and expectations for behaviour onto humans (Connell 2005: 22). Thus, expectations for women (to be feminine) and for men (to be masculine) differ. So how do Japanese children learn their gender?

The home environment plays an important role in teaching children gender distinction. Hidaka (2010) has collected data from salarymen born since the Second World War regarding gendered practices in their upbringing. Some responses seemed nearly constant through all the cohorts, revealing just how widespread such gendered practices are. For example, almost every participant stated that at meal times their father always sat in the seat facing the television and was the person who chose what the family watched;[10] their mother prepared the food and sat in the seat nearest to the kitchen. The rest of the family could not begin eating before their father, and their father often had additional dishes just for himself, such as *sashimi* (Hidaka 2010: 23). Such practices imply to children that their father is held in high esteem, whereas their mother is placed in the position of serving him.

To what extent is this gender distinction reinforced in Japanese schools? Following observations of two primary schools, Peter Cave states that 'gender stereotyping and discrimination were far less evident [...] than in Japanese society more generally' (Cave 2007: 153). While he accepts that gender distinction certainly existed in these schools, it was often adult gender distinction which was most emphasised. For example, all children in one school had

---

[10] Of course this only applies to the cohorts young enough to have had televisions in their households as a child.

a health record entitled *Boshi kenkō techō* (Mother and child health diary), thus assuming mothers, and not fathers, would always fulfill such a role. However, gender-exclusionary practices were never observed in the behaviour of children themselves. Cave points to research in British schools which found high instances of such practices, for example male pupils refusing to allow their female peers to play football with them during break time. Cave never observed such behaviour in these Japanese primary schools. On the contrary, both sexes welcomed and accommodated the other during play (Cave 2007: 157–165).

Thus, Hidaka and Cave have both discovered that many of the gender lessons taught to children in the home and school are for their *adult* roles. The interviewees in Taga Futoshi's research offered similar narratives of their childhood. For example, interviewee Kenji states that before his last couple of years in high school, he never thought about manliness and womanliness ('*otoko-rashisa ya onna-rashisa ni tsuite toku ni kangaeta koto wa naku ...*') (Taga 2006: 56). This could be explained by the fact that the behaviour expected of adults is stressed to children to a greater extent as the child moves from primary to middle to high school (Fukuzawa 1994: 61). Literature on Japanese middle and high schools points to the 'marked sex differentiation of adult roles' as the key gender difference in these institutions (Rohlen 1983: 309). That is to say, the main issue which divides male and female pupils is their future plans after they have graduated from school education. With male pupils more likely to enter a four-year college, social mechanisms encourage female pupils to instead follow traditionally feminine domestic roles (Yoneyama 1999: 40). In the past, the one element of gender discrimination in the high school curriculum was compulsory home economics for female pupils. The object of this was to craft domesticated women of the future, and thus clearly shows the emphasis on gender roles in *adult* life (Rohlen 1983: 309). Researchers have also cited the lack of female teachers in senior management positions, which reinforces the patriarchal dominance which exists in adult society (Kameda 1987: 110).

The idea that gender roles are more important for adults than children can also be observed in books on etiquette and manners. Such books which are aimed at children generally offer the same advice for boys and girls. In the case of adults, however, differing instructions are often given for men and women. For example, in Figures 2 and 3 children are given advice on being polite at meal times with no gender distinction made. In Figure 2, the boy is encouraged to say 'Pardon me for starting first,' when eating his food before others. In Figure 3, the girl is encouraged to say 'That was delicious, thank you' when she has finished eating. In contrast, in Figure 4 men and women are instructed to behave differently when pouring *sake*. The woman is encouraged to use both hands to pour or receive *sake*, whereas the man is allowed to use only one, without a supporting hand.

Fig. 2 and **3**: Table manners for children (Noguchi 2006: 121, 127).

Japanese children certainly learn their gender and experience gender distinction at school and in the home. Cave points to clear examples such as boys and girls having differently coloured shoe toe-caps and gender separation in class lists (Cave 2007: 157). However, children's gender does not have much influence on their lifestyles at this point in their lives, although they are aware of its existence. Rather, they are shown the grave importance that gender roles have in adult life. Cave's research into *bukatsudō* (school clubs) also illustrates the importance placed on preparing children for adult roles, with a particular emphasis on the world of work for boys (Cave 2004: 396). The arguments in my previous chapter clearly tie in with this point: it seems that only when a Japanese male becomes *shakaijin* do expectations regarding specific gendered practices really become relevant.

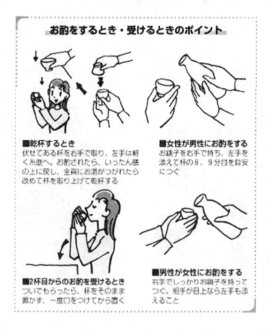

Fig. 4: *Sake* pouring manners for men and women (Iwashita 2002: 100).

Performative Gender and its Problems

If the lifestyles of Japanese males do not become particularly gendered during childhood, how do these males go on to lead highly gendered lifestyles as *shakaijin*? Gender theory can offer help in answering this question. In particular, Judith Butler's theory of performativity offers some key ideas. I will first outline this theory and then apply it to the case of Japanese masculinities.

The word 'performative' was first used by J. L. Austin (1962) in *How to do Things with Words* to express the idea that saying something was doing something. For example, during a wedding ceremony when the bride and groom say 'I do', they are not simply saying words, but also performing an important act – they marry. Later, Judith Butler (1990) applied the term to gender in the context of queer theory in her influential *Gender Trouble*. Her theory states that performativity is 'not a single act, but a repetition and a ritual, which achieves its effects through its naturalisation in the context of a body' (Butler 1999: xv). Butler proposes that acts and gestures 'produce the effect of an internal core or substance' and that such acts and gestures 'are performative in the sense that the essence or identity that they otherwise purport to express are fabrications manufactured and sustained through corporeal signs and other discursive means' (Butler 1990: 173). That is to say, gender is a bodily act (or 'corporeal style') which, when repeated over time, forms an identity. This identity, however, remains a 'cultural fiction' which is only sustained by 'the tacit collective agreement to perform' (Butler 1990: 178–179).

From this explanation, it is difficult to understand what clearly differentiates performativity from performance. If performativity deals with bodily acts, then this cannot be far removed from a theory of performance of gender. Many of those who have employed Butler's theory did indeed read performativity in this manner. This has lead to Butler repeatedly attempting to clarify her theory. She has stressed that performative acts must be repeated to become effective. To give an example of how discourse shapes the categories of gender, she states that the proclamation of 'It's a girl!' at the time of birth begins the process of 'girling' the female subject (Butler 1993a: 2, 107, 232). However, Butler has admitted in the preface to the most recent edition of *Gender Trouble* that 'it is difficult to say what performativity is' (Butler 1999: xiv). In 'Critically Queer' Butler goes on to lament that many have taken her theory to mean that gender is a choice; a construction that one embraces. The idea that 'one goes to the wardrobe of gender and decides with deliberation which gender it will be today' is not the intention of her theory, she argues. She is clear that 'the reduction of perfomativity to performance is a mistake' (Butler 1993b: 21, 24).

This theory, therefore, is problematic and would be difficult to apply to Japanese masculinity, or indeed any society. In a highly critical piece, 'Genre Trouble: (The) Butler Did it', Jon McKenzie attacks Butler for not being consistent with her ideas on performative gender. He argues that in *Gender Trouble* Butler stressed the link between performance and performativity, but in 'Critically Queer' went on to emphasise their difference (McKenzie 1998: 225, 227). I agree that this is the main problem – while performance seems like a useful theory that we might readily apply to Japanese society, performativity seems needlessly complicated and impossible to even clearly define.

Chris Brickell has suggested that it might be possible to 'reclaim the socially constructed agency of performance from the mire of performativity' (Brickell 2005: 24). Brickell criticises Butler for her unclear ideas regarding the subject which is produced by the processes she outlines (for example, the female subject who is 'girled'). Butler continuously shifts her answer to this problem across many inconsistent positions. While at times she emphasises the subject, at others her arguments seem to completely negate the existence of 'agency' (the individual's capability to act purposefully or freely). Such a lack of clarity has resulted in Butler being read as advocating both voluntarism *and* determinism (Brickell 2005: 25–28). Given Butler's extensive writing on subversion of gender practices, who exactly is going to do the subverting if agency does not exist?

So how can performance be reclaimed from this 'mire'? To analyse gender performance from a more sociological perspective, it is necessary to acknowledge some of the factors which Butler does not – social institutions such as gender hierarchy, institutionalised heterosexuality and the state itself. This social order affects men, but men also affect the social order. Such a reflexive view of gender practices allows men to have their subjective agency back. Thus, men who perform masculinity are both constructs and constructors of gender order; they are simultaneously productive and produced (Brickell 2005: 37). While it is important to recognise the ritualised nature of masculinities, to ignore subjective agency is surely a mistake. This theory need not be more complicated than imagining a male actor on stage. He has two parts to play in the production, embodying differing brands of masculinity. The arbitrary nature of these masculinities may be clearly revealed by the fact that the actor is capable of easily switching from one to the other (Reeser 2010: 88). This idea can readily be applied to society, which I will do with the case of Japanese hegemonic masculinity.

Performing Salaryman

Japanese hegemonic masculinity, in the form of the salaryman, may be seen as a performance – one that occurs within the context of strong social pressures to conform to a certain standard of lifestyle and behaviour that is expected of a male *shakaijin* (Dasgupta 2000: 191). If one does not perform in this manner, sanctions, such as not being promoted at work, may result (Murata 2000: 541; Dasgupta 2005: 173). There is a close relationship between the construction of masculinity in Japan and the needs of the state (Low 2003: 91). Dasgupta states that salarymen 'represent state-sponsored, patriarchal, industrial capitalism, disseminated and reinforced very effectively through the instruments of state and society' (Dasgupta 2000: 192). Male *shakaijin* are told how they must perform,[11] and if they do not, they are not thought of as adults, but children (Lunsing 2001: 75).

However, the performance required of salarymen does not only entail broad lifestyle choices such as regular employment and marriage, but also the minutiae of everyday life. Dress should consist of a white shirt, dark business suit and general lack of anything 'flashy' (*hade*) such as accessories. Hair should be of natural colour and neatly cropped. Consumer habits and even body language are tightly regulated. The real crafting of individual males to fit in with the salaryman discourse becomes most important when one ceases to be a student and enters the workforce. A great deal of stress is placed on ridding oneself of *gakusei kibun* (student mentality) and taking on the serious responsibilities of being *shakaijin* (Dasgupta 2000: 193–194). To an extent, we can see this process already beginning during *shūshoku katsudō* (job hunting), which begins in the latter half of the third year at university. This regulated process takes place only once in a person's life and, due to age limitations in recruitment practices, is of grave importance (Mathews 2004: 121–2). When applying for jobs, students often have to write essays such as 'My thoughts on becoming *shakaijin*'. Such preparation, along with regularly attending interviews, results in students slowly beginning their transition to *shakaijin* and the expectations this role demands (Roberson 1995: 307).

There are concrete examples of training and instruction regarding how a man should *perform* when he reaches this stage of his life. In Japan, companies usually recruit at the same time of the year, with inductees (*shinnyūsha'in*) then entering the company in one large group. Before this can occur, an intensive period of induction takes place. This orientation is regarded by companies as an important first step in the process of shaping the ideal *kaisha no*

---

[11] It should be noted that there is an equally important stress placed on women in Japan to perform in a certain way, though in a markedly different way.

ningen (literally 'company person'). Indeed, virtually all companies, regardless of their size or location, dedicate considerable resources to the training of inductees in this way. These courses often take place outside of the company itself, sometimes in particularly isolated surroundings. This emphasises the importance of induction into the company as a watershed moment in the individual's life. They enter the course as a student and emerge as a newly-born *shakaijin* (Dasgupta 2000: 195).

A plethora of self-help literature on how to perform correctly also exists. Suzuki Kenji's *Otoko wa 20 dai ni nani o nasubeki ka: ningen no kihon o mi ni tsukeru tame ni* (What should a man do in his twenties? A guide to learning the basics of being human) tells the reader what he is required to do before he reaches the age of thirty and how he should do it (quoted in Dasgupta 2000: 196). Thus, men are being instructed on how to live up to the appropriate ideals of masculinity through certain performances. The content of this book, for example, runs from table manners, to workplace tips, to advice on marriage and sex. Men's magazines deal with equally minute issues, such as the proper way to wear a suit, whilst also providing instructions on 'how to perform heterosexuality correctly', with detailed advice on everything from the advantages and disadvantages of a relationship with an older woman, to explicit guides for sexual encounters (Dasgupta 2000: 196–197). This is very telling because magazines aimed at younger males (pre-*shakaijin*) are often far more ambiguous with some of the sexual imagery that they use. Magazines such as *Men's Non-no* often allow for non-heterosexual readings. The salarymen-targeted men's magazines, however, are insistently and even aggressively heterosexual. Their message is that to perform successfully as a salaryman, one must perform successfully as a heterosexual (Dasgupta 2000: 198).

The fact that instruction regarding correct masculine performance is necessary betrays the instability of what is often viewed as an impenetrable discourse. The interviewee in Mathews' *ikigai* research who stated that he hated his work but *had* to have it as his *ikigai*, because to have family as his *ikigai* would seem effeminate (*memeshii*), exemplifies this idea. While his true wishes might be different, he feels he is under pressure to perform a particular type of masculinity which places work as his *ikigai* (Mathews 2003: 117). The advertising of *genki* drinks displays a similar pattern. It is performance of masculinity in its most literal sense: famous men, who are known not to be salarymen in their real lives, perform this hegemonic masculine ideal for the cameras (Roberson 2005: 370). Though in society there might not be a camera, it is a stage nonetheless, and Japanese males are performing as salarymen just like these actors. The only difference is that, while an actor can step down from a stage, such a rejection of performance is not possible on the social stage.

Conclusion

While Japanese children certainly learn their gender in the home and at school, this gender distinction does not markedly impact their lifestyles during childhood. Rather, the gender 'lessons' they are taught strongly emphasise adult gender roles, with clearly distinct expectations for adult men and women. These adult roles are more strongly emphasised as a child moves from primary to middle to high school, as they are also moving closer to adult life. Gender theory can explain this phenomenon with theories of performance, which suggest that gender is not embodied in identity, but rather is an act which is performed by the subject. Such masculine performance can clearly be seen in salarymen who must conform to a rigid set of demands regarding their lifestyles, even when they do not always wish to do so. Popular instruction manuals regarding correct performance by these salarymen illustrate the arbitrary nature of this hegemonic masculinity. It is clear, however, that some young Japanese males, such as *sō-shokukei danshi*, are not performing as is expected and are thus subverting hegemonic masculinity.

HEGEMONY CHALLENGED

Subverting Gender Order

While masculine performance may reinforce the gender order in a society, it may also resist hegemonic social arrangements. In this way, subversion may add and proliferate newly permissible ways of being gendered. How one understands oneself as a gendered subject is usually conditioned through particular 'frames' that structure social intercourse – subversion is an act which slightly nudges these acceptable frames. This re-framing may be taken up, disseminated and further modified through interaction. While extending this throughout a whole society may prove difficult, cracks within hegemonic patterns may permit certain acts which lead to a reconfiguring of acceptable masculine performance (Brickell 2005: 38–40).

Such cracks have appeared and opened very large in Japanese society in the last two decades. Poor economic conditions have resulted in the salaryman model of masculinity being problematised (Dasgupta 2000: 199). During the bubble period in the late 1980s, large companies recruited heavily from high school leavers and university graduates, but when the bubble burst in the early 1990s this smooth transition from education to work was disrupted. From its peak in 1992, the virtually total employment of school leavers continued to decline, and high schools and vocational colleges were no longer able to guarantee job offers from employers for their students (Hidaka 2010: 105–108). Thus, subscribing to the salary-man model became far less appealing and the features of this model, such as permanent employment and seniority-based pro-motions, became nearly impossible to sustain. For large numbers of middle-aged males who suddenly found themselves without what had seemed to be secure employment, the issues went beyond simply losing their job – their very identity as fathers, as providers and as *men* was being called into question. One outcome of this has been an overall questioning of Japanese masculinity in a way that would have been difficult to imagine in earlier decades (Dasgupta 2003: 131). If there was a time for the framework of acceptable masculinities to shift in Japan, this was surely it.

The Emergence of Freeters

Coinciding with this economic decline was the emergence of new forms of employment. The term 'freeter' was coined in the late 1980s, while the economy was still booming, and refers to people who refused to become permanent employees, instead engaging in part-time or temporary work. These were people who deliberately chased alternative careers, such as the dramatic arts or music, but needed money to fund such ambitions in the meantime (Kosugi 2006). The word itself (*furiitā* in Japanese) is a compound of the English 'free' and the German 'Arbeiter' (worker; Hidaka 2010: 107). The government takes this term seriously and has an official definition of 'freeters' as those aged fifteen to thirty-four, who are neither in education, nor are married women, and who work part-time (Taga 2006: 81). The number of freeters increased dramatically after the economic downturn, from 1.83 million in 1992 to as high as 4.17 million in 2001 – about one fifth of this demographic (Mōri 2005: 22).[12] This was a dramatic shift in employment practices and, due to the situation before the downturn, has affected men the most (Taga 2006: 76).

There are two discourses on the motivation (or lack thereof) of freeters. The media and popular discourse has largely portrayed them as lazy and work-shy. Academics, however, have pointed to the difficult economic situation as evidence that freeters do not

---

[12] It should be noted that in some texts this number is roughly half the size because certain organisations define only those who have *actively sought* non-regular or part-time work as freeters, thereby excluding those who have given up looking for a job because of a variety of reasons (Cook 2012). I have used the larger number because it is surely important to recognise both groups.

necessarily *want* to shun permanent employment, but have no other option (Mōri 2005: 22). There is also evidence to suggest a third option – those who wish to work, but on terms different from the permanent employment style typified by the salaryman. There are freeters who actively choose part-time or casual work, as they are seeking flexible hours, limited responsibility, and jobs that are interesting and personally satisfying, as well as offering an easy entry into and exit from employment. Many freeters speak of having an aversion to 'corporate culture' and being tied to one company (Hidaka 2010: 109). The media has recently begun to report this point too, for example the *Asahi Shimbun* has cited university students during *shūshoku katsudō* who question whether they should just be freeters instead (*furiitā demo ii ka*). One student is quoted as saying '*jibun no tokusei ga ikaseru shigoto ni tsukitai*' ('I want to do a job where I can make good use of my personal qualities') when discussing why he might prefer to be a freeter (*Asahi Shimbun* 2011). Thus, to view all freeters as victims of economic stagnation, or as lazy and work-shy, would be short-sighted. A 2000 Japan Institute of Labour survey found that roughly half of freeters sought a full-time job but gave up, with the other half actively pursuing a freeter lifestyle from the outset (Kosugi 2001: 58).

Honda Yuki has followed this line of argument, suggesting that to see all freeters as victims is too simplistic (Honda 2005: 5). Her interviews with freeters give us valuable insight into the reasons why some young people have chosen this form of employment. One male respondent failed his university entrance exam and therefore took up a job in a restaurant while studying to retake it. However, he enjoyed the job so much that he gave up studying and stayed in the service sector, aiming to work in a hotel. Another respondent claimed that life as a salaryman is not a happy one, as you are driven too hard. Meanwhile a third stated that regular workers have to be 'perfect human beings' and he could not handle the responsibility that would come with such employment (Honda 2005: 12, 22). In her interviews, Emma Cook found the same attitude, with one interviewee stating 'I could never be a salaryman. I think that it's better for people to do jobs they like' (Cook 2012). Thus, while economic decline has most likely triggered this phenomenon, other factors are perpetuating it today.

Working habits are key to my discussion of Japanese masculinity due to the importance regular, permanent employment has had in hegemonic discourses. If the employment practices of Japanese males are changing, so too is their masculine performance. Such attitudinal changes in younger generations can be seen as an attempt to transform hegemonic masculinity (Ishii-Kuntz 2003: 201). Some have argued that because males who do not partake in regular employment are not considered *shakaijin*, but rather are considered to be almost like children, this phenomenon of the freeter lifestyle is a prolonging of adolescence (Honda 2005: 23). Taga specifically refers to this phase as '*posuto-seinenki*' (post-adolescence), which takes place before adulthood. He refers to the constituents of this phase as '*otoko ni narenai dansei*' ('males who cannot become men') (Taga 2006: 76). Cook (2012) has extended this argument to discuss a period of 'liminality' and suggests that the early twenties operate as a 'liminal space' where youths are not expected to be adults.

This theory adds weight to my argument regarding the importance of gender roles becoming relevant at the *shakaijin* stage of life. However, Cook also speculates that the constituents of this 'liminal space' will eventually 'grow up', and conform to hegemonic gender roles. This view does not fully acknowledge the gravity of the changes we are seeing. Whether the causes lie with the poor economy or personal choice, it is unlikely that either will suddenly return to the previous status quo and the hegemonic masculinity described above will regain full dominance. Cook, perhaps, betrays her point by stating that the average age of male freeters is increasing, thereby showing that these men are, in fact, not 'growing out' of this lifestyle (Cook 2012). Instead, I suggest that these developments have allowed for a greater range of voices to be heard, with other 'alternative' masculinities, which existed in the shadow of hegemonic masculinity, becoming more visible (Dasgupta 2003: 131). The performance of these alternative masculinities is becoming more common, and this may eventually result in a redefining of how male *shakaijin* are permitted to behave.

Marriage as a Personal Choice

Despite the vital importance of marriage in hegemonic discourses on masculinity, this too is an area where change has been visible in recent years. Marriage rates in Japan are in decline, while alternative relationship structures (such as cohabitation without marriage) and singledom in middle-age are on the rise (Sugimoto 2003: 173). Such 'alternative' relationships and bachelorhood are often still heavily criticised, however. For men, the pressure to marry from superiors in their workplace and from their family can be strong. As a result, younger people who have opted for such lifestyles sometimes hide this fact from co-workers or even family members (Tokuhiro 2010: 108).

While much of the discourse on this issue centres around women, many of whom are said to be choosing careers over marriage, it is important to emphasise that men are also actively participating in this change. For example, many young Japanese males who lead freeter lifestyles acknowledge the impact this has on their chances of marriage. One of the main reasons that social perceptions of male freeters in particular are so poor is that they are not seen as capable of providing for a family or being responsible enough for such a task – even female freeters often state that they would never marry a male freeter. Being aware of this issue, yet still actively pursuing such a lifestyle, illustrates a rejection of traditional expectations by these men (Cook 2012).

My own interviewees often had a similar attitude. For example, Honda-kun (who, incidentally, did not identify as *sō-shokukei*) stated that he, and many of his peers, did not see the necessity (*hitsuyōsei*) of marriage as much as his parents' generation. While for the latter it might have been obvious (*atarimae*), for him and his peers it is '*kojin no sentaku*' ('the choice of the individual') with no particular judgment of this choice as good or bad. Such ideas were very common in the male students I interviewed. Even those who stated that they had a stable relationship and thought they would probably get married one day were clear that this was not necessarily the 'correct' choice, and that others who did not marry were not 'incorrect', but rather that everyone was free to lead the life they wanted to. Thus, while it is not the case by any means that all young Japanese men despise marriage, it can be seen that more are deciding against this lifestyle. While those who make this choice are often still heavily criticised by their seniors, the feelings of their own generation are much more ambivalent, with lifestyle choices being seen as entirely up to the individual and not the business of others to comment on.

Beautified Men

Changes are also visible in male beauty practices. The young, beautified male is an image which has become more and more commonplace in Japanese society in recent years (Iida 2005: 56). Given the performance required of males subscribing to hegemonic masculinity in relation to dress and appearance, the popularity of the beautified male may also be seen as a subversion of hegemonic masculinity. Kimura Takuya, member of the boy band 'SMAP' and an extremely popular 'idol' (*aidoru*) and actor, was the first man to advertise make-up targeted at women in a cosmetics campaign launched in 1996. [13] The campaign was very influential and triggered a new wave of 'beautiful men' used in such advertising, both for cosmetics aimed at women and the increasing number of those aimed at men (Ezaki 1997: 19).

---

[13] See: http://v.youku.com/v_show/id_XODI1OTY5MDg=.htmlP.

Laura Miller has analysed this new wave of beautified men in terms of masculinity. She argues that efforts at body and beauty transformation suggest that the ideological sphere of masculinity has widened to include a greater diversity of physical styles. She does not see current male beauty practices as a kind of feminisation of men, but rather a shift to beautification being a component of masculinity (Miller 2006: 126). Thus, performing a masculinity which embraces consumption of beauty products is becoming more acceptable and even encouraged by young males themselves. Some have argued that this is not a new form of masculinity at all, but rather a resurrection of Heian period (794–1185) ideals of male beauty, particularly encapsulated in *The Tale of Genji* (ca. 1008) (Hirota 1997: 62). Male characters in Lady Murasaki's work represent the ideal man of that time as sensitive, emotional and beautiful, with Genji, himself, being the pinnacle (Morris 1994: 158). However, as the majority of contemporary fashion trends embrace modernity and the avant-garde, an historical framework is not particularly useful in understanding the issue (Iida 2005: 58). It would be farfetched to suggest that there is a concerted effort among young Japanese males to emulate the ways of Heian Japan and thus I do not read the current phenomenon as such.

Instead, I propose that the employment of these aesthetic practices by young males is an assertion of an alternative masculine performance which is made possible by distancing themselves from hegemonic patterns. Rather than a feminisation of men, it is a silent refutation of imposed ideologies and cultural expectations; a counter-hegemonic practice which is challenging the conventional values and ideals of hegemonic masculinity (Iida 2005: 57).

Conclusion

The decline of corporate masculine culture in Japan since the end of the bubble period has provided young males with the opportunity to explore and assert new gender identities (Iida 2005: 61).

These are males who perform self as their *ikigai* without feeling pressured to perform work as their *ikigai* (Mathews 2003: 119). Conditions of late capitalism have been instrumental in this process, with the development of an urban culture that encourages males to participate in the previously feminine sphere of conspicuous consumption. Marriage rates have begun to decline and young males seem to view marriage as more of a personal choice than a necessity. Shifts in employment practices have also allowed more individualistic and creative job routes to become permissible, whereas the traditional salaryman route has become less desirable (Dasgupta 2000: 200). Problematisation of the latter's performance has opened up the possibility of destabilising and subverting this hegemonic discourse, with new masculinities, which place importance on the self, becoming more acceptable. *Sōshokukei danshi* are a clear example of a new masculinity which encapsulate this desire to place the self centre stage.

CONCLUSION: HERBIVORES AS SUBVERTERS

The similarities between the lifestyle of *sōshokukei danshi* discussed in my first chapter and the increasing subversion of hegemonic masculinity by young Japanese males discussed in my fourth chapter are clear. I have argued that, in fact, they overlap greatly. That is to say, in recent years a shift in masculine performance has begun to occur in young males, and in order to more easily discuss the phenomenon, the media have latched on to the term '*sōshokukei danshi*' to describe a general societal shift. Thus, to an extent, the very idea of *sōshokukei danshi* is a fabrication. That is not to say that the attributes given to *sōshokukei danshi* and the changes in masculine performance they are said to embody are not real. Rather, the particular categorising of one young male as 'herbivore' and one as 'carnivore' is artificial. One 'herbivore' male does not necessarily embody every feature attributed to this grouping. Rather, the situation is far more fluid, as would be expected of gradual change in a society, with the performance of Japanese young males, in general, shifting.

But why is this societal shift being seen as such a crisis of masculinity in Japan? Why are these new men causing such moral panic (see *Times* 2009; *Nihon Keizai Shimbun* 2010 etc)? Historically Japanese society has supported strong hegemonic masculine ideals. After the Second World War, these masculine ideals, embodied by the salaryman, were used to rebuild Japan (Napier 2011: 164). While hegemonic femininity placed women as wives and mothers,[14] men had to perform two main roles – to support their family through earnings and to work hard for their company. In this way, both were supporting the nation. Men helped the economy grow; women cared for the current generation and

---

[14] It should be noted that women have always participated in the Japanese workforce, often working before marriage and returning to part-time work when their children have grown up. This was never part of their gender ideology, however.

raised the next generation. And together, by producing children, they helped to further the nation's growth (Dasgupta 2003: 121). Thus, we can see that performance of hegemonic gender ideology has, in Japanese post-war history, come to stabilise, support and build up the nation. Hegemonic masculinity has placed men as *daikokubashira* not just for their own family, but for Japan itself. In this way, men have been conditioned to perform in a way which dedicates their lives to the making of a prosperous nation (Mathews 2003: 111).

For many years, this performance achieved tangible results. Japan rose from its battered post-war state to become the world's second-largest economy within three decades. Salarymen who gave their all for the company saw the fruits of their labour and new generations rose to the challenge of matching these results. Men had a clearly defined purpose, and to not perform in this manner seemed unthinkable (Mathews 2004: 124). When the economy faltered, this system started to crumble and hegemonic masculinity was problematised. However, such rigid gender roles were *still* tied to the good of the nation. Therefore, when a crisis of the nation occurs, such as Japan's current problems with its economy, aging society and low birthrate to name just a few, it is also inexorably linked to a crisis in gender roles.

The current subversion of hegemonic masculinity, embodied in particular by *sōshokukei danshi*, is, from the perspective of older generations, exacerbating (or even causing) this crisis. Such new men are thought to be not particularly keen on finding a girlfriend or having sex – thus, the low birth rate can be blamed on them. They do not like to make expensive purchases, but rather concentrate on smaller, aesthetic treatments and items – thus, poor consumption rates damaging the economy can be blamed on them. They do not want to dedicate their lives full-time to a company, but rather pursue their dreams and ambitions, which often involves working part-time or in non-regular work – thus Japan's stagnation can be blamed on them. This is all framed by a general accusation of selfishness committed by these new men, as they are not living for the nation, or even for a company or family, but instead are living for themselves. This individualistic attitude is truly the antithesis of Japanese hegemonic masculinity, which has placed the interests of the nation at its core.

There are two sides to this issue, however. While for older generations this may be a time of crisis, for the herbivore boys, who have grown up during a period of Japan's history so very different from their fathers, it is a time of opportunity. The hegemonic masculinity which has tied men's responsibilities to the development of the nation no longer applies. On the contrary, many of these young males have grown up despising their father's path in life. Thus, a situation in which it was once unthinkable to subvert hegemonic masculinity has become one in which *not* subverting it, at least partially, is now unthinkable. Even those who might desire the lifestyle of a salaryman, no longer see the benefits of such a lifestyle (Mathews 2004: 124, 128).

With this particular performance of masculinity less relevant and less appealing, the door has been opened for these new men to concentrate on themselves. While some may see it as selfishness, these young males are enjoying the opportunity to perform in a way which (they believe) is true to themselves, just like the interviewee in my first chapter who stated '*boku wa boku*'; 'I am what I am.'

Chris Deacon

REFERENCES

Allison, Anne (1994). *Nightwork: Sexuality, Pleasure, and Corporate Masculinity in a Tokyo Hostess Club*. Chicago: University of Chicago Press.

Artesia (2009). *Sōshokukei danshi ni koi sureba: In Love With a Herbivore Boy*. Tōkyō: Media Factory.

Austin, J. L. (1962). *How to Do Things with Words*. Cambridge, MA: Harvard University Press.

Brickell, Chris (2005). 'Masculinities, Performativity and Subversion: A Sociological Reappraisal', *Men and Masculinities* 8/1, pp. 24–43.

Butler, Judith (1990). *Gender Trouble: Feminism and the Subversion of Identity*. London: Routledge.

Butler, Judith (1993a). *Bodies That Matter: On the Discursive Limits of 'Sex'*. London: Routledge.

Butler, Judith (1993b). 'Critically Queer', *Journal of Lesbian and Gay Studies* 1/1, pp. 17–32.

Butler, Judith (1999). *Gender Trouble: Feminism and the Subversion of Identity*. Second edition, with a new preface. London: Routledge.

Cave, Peter (2004). 'Bukatsudō: The Educational Role of Japanese School Clubs', *Journal of Japanese Studies* 30/2, pp. 383–415.

Cave, Peter (2007). *Primary School in Japan: Self, Individuality and Learning in Elementary Education*. Abingdon: Routledge.

Connell, R. W. (2005). *Masculinities*. Second edition. Cambridge: Polity Press.

Cook, Emma (2012). 'Still a Child? Liminality and the Construction of Youthful Masculinities in Japan', Karen Brison and Susan Dewey (eds) *Super Girls, Gangstas, Freeters, and Xenomaniacs: Gender and Modernity in Youth Cultures*. Syracuse, NY: Syracuse University Press, chapter 3.

Dasgupta, Romit (2000). 'Performing Masculinities? The "Salary-man" at Work and Play', *Journal of Japanese Studies* 20/2, pp.189–200.

Dasgupta, Romit (2003). 'Creating Corporate Warriors: The "Salaryman" and Masculinity in Japan', Kam Louie and Morris Low (eds) *Asian Masculinities: The Meaning and Practice of Manhood in China and Japan.* London: Routledge, pp. 118–134.

Dasgupta, Romit (2005). 'Salarymen Doing Straight. Heterosexual Men and the Dynamics of Gender Conformity', Mark Mc-Lelland and Romit Dasgupta (eds) *Genders, Transgenders and Sexualities in Japan.* Oxford: Routledge, pp. 168–182.

Ezaki Rie (1997). 'Otoko o sasō onna ni narō' (Let's become women who seduce men), Nakano Kuniko et al. (eds) *Otoko tarashi ron* (On handling men). Tōkyō: Heibon-sha, pp. 19–24.

Frühstück, Sabine (2007). *Uneasy Warriors: Gender, Memory, and Popular Culture in the Japanese Army.* Berkley: University of California Press.

Fukasawa Maki (2009). *Sōshoku danshi sedai* (The herbivore boys generation). Tōkyō: Kōbun-sha.

Fukuzawa, Rebecca (1994). 'The Path to Adulthood According to Japanese Middle Schools', *Journal of Japanese Studies* 20/1, pp. 61–86.

Hidaka Tomoko (2010). *Salaryman Masculinity. Continuity and Change in Hegemonic Masculinity in Japan.* Leiden: Brill.

Hirota Akiko (1997). 'The Tale of Genji: From Heian Classic to Heian Comic', *Journal of Popular Culture* 31/2, pp. 29–68.

Honda Yuki (2005). 'Freeters: Young Atypical Workers in Japan', *Japan Labor Review* 2/3, pp. 5–25.

Ichibanchō (2009). *Sōshoku danshi no shindansho* (Herbivore boy diagnosis manual). Tōkyō: Takarajima-sha.

Iida Yumiko (2005). 'Beyond the "Feminisation of Masculinity". Transforming Patriarchy with the "Feminine" in Contemporary Japanese Youth Culture', *Inter-Asia Cultural Studies* 6/1, pp. 56–74.

Inui Akiko (2005). 'Why Freeter and NEET are Misunderstood: Recognizing the New Precarious Conditions of Japanese Youth', *Social Work and Society Journal* 3/2, pp. 244–251.

IPSS (2011). *Dai 14 kai shusshō dōkō kihon chōsa* (Number 14: Investigation into the basis of birth trends). http://www.ipss.go.jp/ps-doukou/j/doukou14_s/doukou14_s.asp (accessed 25 February 2012).

Ishii-Kuntz, Masako (2003). 'Balancing Fatherhood and Work: Emergence of Diverse Masculinities in Contemporary Japan', James Roberson and Suzuki Nobue (eds) *Men and Masculinities in Contemporary Japan. Dislocating the Salaryman Doxa*. London: Routledge, pp. 198–216.

Itō Kimio (1996). *Dansei-gaku nyūmon* (Introduction to Men's Studies). Tōkyō: Sakushin-sha.

Iwashita Noriko (2002). *Manā jiten* (Encyclopedia of manners). Tōkyō: Natsume-sha.

Kameda Atsuko (1987). *Onna no me de miru. Kōza josei gaku* (Seeing through a woman's eyes: lectures on Women's Studies). Tōkyō: Keisō shobō.

Kosugi Reiko (2001). 'The Transition from School to Work in Japan: Understanding the Increase in Freeter and Jobless Youth', *Japan Labor Review* 1/1, pp. 52–67.

Kosugi Reiko (2006). 'Youth Employment in Japan's Economic Recovery: Freeters and NEETs', *The Asia-Pacific Journal* http://www.japanfocus.org/-Kosugi-Reiko/2022 (accessed 25 February 2012).

Low, Morris (2003). 'The Emperor's Sons Go to War: Competing Masculinities in Modern Japan', Kam Louie and Morris Low (eds) *Asian Masculinities: The Meaning and Practice of Manhood in China and Japan*. London: Routledge, pp. 81–99.

Lunsing, Wim (2001). *Beyond Common Sense: Negotiating Constructions of Sexuality and Gender in Contemporary Japan*. London: Kegan Paul International.

Mason, Michele (2011). 'Empowering the Would-be Warrior: Bushidō and the Gendered Bodies of the Japanese Nation',

Sabine Frühstück and Anne Walthall (eds) *Recreating Japanese Men*. Berkley: University of California Press, pp. 68–90.

Mathews, Gordon (2003). 'Can 'a Real Man' Live for his Family? *Ikigai* and Masculinity in Today's Japan', James Roberson and Suzuki Nobue (eds) *Men and Masculinities in Contemporary Japan: Dislocating the Salaryman Doxa*. London: Routledge, pp. 108–125.

Mathews, Gordon (2004). 'Seeking a Career, Finding a Job: How Young People Enter and Resist the Japanese World of Work', Gordon Mathews and Bruce White (eds) *Japan's Changing Generations: Are Young People Creating a New Society?* Abingdon: Routledge, pp. 121–136.

McKenzie, Jon (1998). 'Genre Trouble. (The) Butler Did It', Peggy Phelan and Jill Lane (eds) *The Ends of Performance*. New York: New York University Press, pp. 217–235.

McLelland, Mark (2005). 'Salarymen Doing Queer: Gay Men and the Heterosexual Public Sphere', Mark McLelland and Romit Dasgupta (eds) *Genders, Transgenders and Sexualities in Japan*. Oxford: Routledge, pp. 96–110.

Miller, Laura (2006). *Beauty Up: Exploring Contemporary Japanese Body Aesthetics*. Berkeley: University of California Press.

Mōri Yoshitaka (2008). 'Culture = Politics: The Emergence of New Cultural Forms of Protest in the Age of the Freeter', *Inter-Asia Cultural Studies* 6/1, pp. 17–29.

Morioka Masahiro (2008). *Sōshokukei danshi no ren'ai gaku* (Lessons in love for herbivore men). Tōkyō: Media Factory.

Morioka Masahiro (2009). *Saigo no koi wa sōshokukei danshi ga motte kuru* (A herbivore man will bring your last love). Tōkyō: Magajin hausu.

Morioka Masahiro (2011). '"Sōshoku kei danshi' no genshō gakuteki kōsatsu' (A phenomenological enquiry into 'herbivore boys'), *The Review of Life Studies* 1, pp. 13–28.

Morris, Ivan (1994). *The World of the Shining Prince: Court Life in Ancient Japan*. New York: Kodansha.

Murata Yohei (2000). 'Chūnen shinguru dansei o sogai suru basho' (Places where middle-aged single men feel alienated), *Jinbun Chirigaku* 52/6, pp. 533–551.

Napier, Susan (2011). 'Where Have All the Salarymen Gone?', Sabine Frühstück and Anne Walthall (eds) *Recreating Japanese Men*. Berkley: University of California Press, pp. 154–176.

Nitobe Inazō (1905). *Bushidō, The Soul of Japan. An Exposition of Japanese Thought*. Republished online by 'Forgotten Books' (forgottenbooks.org).

Noguchi Yoshihiro (2006). *Shōgakusei made ni mi ni tsukeru: kodomo no sahō* (Children's etiquette to learn up to primary school age). Tōkyō: PHP.

Okuda Hiromi (2009). *Sōshokukei bijinesuman no tame no sutoresu-furii shigoto jutsu: 'Stress-Free' Lifehacks For Herbivorous Businessmen*. Tokyo: Soshi-sha.

Reeser, Todd (2010). *Masculinities in Theory. An Introduction*. Chichester: Blackwell.

Roberson, James (1995). 'Becoming *Shakaijin*: Working-Class Reproduction in Japan', *Ethnology* 34/2, pp. 293–313.

Roberson, James (2005). 'Fight!! Ippatsu!! "Genki" Energy Drinks and the Marketing of Masculine Ideology in Japan', *Men and Masculinities* 7/4, pp. 365–384.

Rohlen, Thomas (1983). *Japan's High Schools*. Berkley: University of California Press.

Sugimoto Yoshio (2003). *An Introduction to Japanese Society*. Second edition. Cambridge: Cambridge University Press.

Taga Futoshi (2006). *Otoko-rashisa no shakai-gaku* (The sociology of manliness). Kyōto: Sekaishiso Seminar.

Takeuchi Kumiko (2010). *Sōshoku danshi 0.95 no kabe* (Herbivore men. The 0.95 wall). Tōkyō: Bungei Shunju.

Toivonen, Tuukka and Imoto Yuki (2012). 'Making Sense of Youth Problems', Roger Goodman, Yuki Imoto and Tuukka Toivonen (eds) *A Sociology of Japanese Youth. From Returnees to Neets*. Abingdon: Routledge, pp. 1–29.

Tokuhiro Yoko (2010). *Marriage in Contemporary Japan*. London: Routledge.

Ushikubo Megumi (2008). *Sōshokukei danshi 'ojōman' ga Nihon o kaeru* ('Girly' herbivore men will change Japan). Tōkyō: Kōdansha.

Ushikubo Megumi (2009). *Sōshokukei danshi no tori atsukai setsumeisho* (Herbivore men user manual). Tōkyō: Bijinesu-sha.

Watanabe Kōji (2010). *Sōshokukei danshi X niku shoku joshi: dochira ga sodatsu ka?* (Herbivore man X carnivore woman: which will be raised?). Tōkyō: First Press.

Yoneyama Shoko (1999). *The Japanese High School: Silence and Resistance*. London: Routledge.

Newspaper Articles and Radio Programmes

Asahi Shimbun (1996). 'Otoko to onna tokedashita' (Men and women have blended), 13 April.

Asahi Shimbun (2011). 'Shūshoku sensen, hikari wa doko ni 'nen'nai ni wa kimetai'' (Job hunting front line, where is the light for 'I want to decide within the year'), 18 November.

Bloomberg (2009). 'Dude Looks Like a Lady in Our Recessionary Times'. http://www.bloomberg.com/apps/news?pid=news archive&sid=aEMEP10Ama6g.

Clarín (2009). '¿La recesión alienta a los 'hombres herbívoros'?' (Is the recession encouraging 'herbivore men'?). http://edant.clarin.com/suplementos/zona/2009/07/05/z-01952827.htm.

Guardian, The (2011). 'Japan Leads the Way in Sexless Love'. http://www.guardian.co.uk/commentisfree/2011/dec/27/japan-men-sexless-love.

Huffington Post, The (2011) 'Japan Population Decline'. http:// huffingtonpost.com/2012/01/30/japan-population-decline-youth-no-sex_n_1242014.html.

Japan Times, The (2009a) 'Blurring the Boundaries'. http://www. japantimes.co.jp/text/fl20090510x1.html.

Japan Times, The (2009b). '"Herbivorous Men" are New Consumer Kings'. http://www.japantimes.co.jp/text/nn20090716f2.html.

Lifestudies.org (*un-dated*). *Special Report No. 4. Herbivore Men*. http://www.lifestudies.org/specialreport04.html.

Nikkei Business (2006). 'Dai 5 kai Sōshoku danshi' (Number 5: Herbivore boys). http://business.nikkeibp.co.jp/article/skillup/20061005/111136.

Nihon Keizai Shimbun (2010). 'Musuko ga kekkon dekinai kamo ... "Sōshokukei" ni oya yakimoki' (Maybe my son isn't capable of marriage …. Parents' worries for 'herbivores'). http://www.nikkei.com/article/DGXZZO15036200R20C10A9000000/.

NPR (2009). 'In Japan, "Herbivore" Boys Subvert Ideas of Manhood'. http:://www.npr.org/templates/story/story.php?storyID=120696816.

Reuters (2009). 'Japan's 'Herbivore' Men Shun Corporate Life, Sex'. http://www.reuters.com/article/2009/07/27/us-japan-herbivores-idUSTRE56Q0C220090727.

SPA! (2011) 'PlayStation Vita hatsubai! Gaiken wa sōshokukei demo kinō wa nikushokukei' (PlayStation Vita launch! It looks herbivorous but its features are carnivorous). http://nikkan-spa.jp/105088.

Telegraph, The (2009). 'Third of Young Japanese Men not Interested in Sex'. http://www.telegraph.co.uk/news/worldnews/asia/japan/8257400/Third-of-young-Japanese-men-not-interested-in-sex.html.

Times, The (2011). 'Girly Men of Japan Just Want to Have Fun'. http://www.timesonline.co.uk/tol/news/world/asia/article6898611.ece.

Yomiuri Online, The (2009) 'Antei shikō no "sōshokukei danshi"' (Stability-orientated 'herbivore men'). http://www.yomiuri.co.jp/komachi/news/mixnews/20090217ok02.htm

All online sources accessed 25 February 2012.

5 Resistance and Assimilation

Medical and Legal Transgender Identities in Japan

Nicola McDermott

Supervisor: Brigitte Steger (2011)

Table of Contents

I would like to thank Dr Steger for her enthusiasm and
help throughout the research and writing of this dissertation.

INTRODUCTION

In October 2009, male-to-female transgender 'talent'[15] Haruna Ai, a Japanese national, won the title of Miss International Queen at a transgender beauty contest in Pattaya, Thailand. Using the media attention, she called for Japan to become more accepting and tolerant towards the transgender community. She noted that transgender people in Thailand

> can work at hotels and restaurants with no problem [...].
> Even after I had a sex change operation at the age of 19
> [...] I encountered many, many obstacles [in Japan] that
> constantly made me realise I wasn't a woman.

She recalled being rejected five times in a row when applying to rent apartments in Japan, as the owners felt neighbours might object (*AFP News* 3 December 2009). Haruna's plea for tolerance high-lights some of the areas where the lives of transgender people are complicated in Japan because of their gender identity.

Why should living as the gender opposite to the one assigned to you at birth pose so many problems in fundamental parts of your life? In this dissertation I detail the current standing of transgender rights in Japan, mapping the development of the transgender community from the post-war period, through the legalisation of sex reassignment surgery (hereafter SRS) and the passing of a law allowing for legal gender change in July 2003 (Ishida 2008: 23). More specifically, I will investigate how the state and medical establishment frame a homogenous transgender identity in Japan, and to show how adequately (or inadequately) this represents the variety of indigenous categories that exist. Though medical and legal recognition of the transsexual identity since 1996 has arguably benefitted the lives of those who are well described by

---

[15] A 'talent' or '*tarento*' in Japan is a media personality who regularly appears in entertainment shows on television, usually with some sort of gimmick like a costume or trademark phrase.

these discourses, I will also highlight cases where they have regulated or marginalised more complex and variant identities.

Although interest in 'marginal' sexual and gender identities in Japan has been increasing in recent years, scholarship in English on Japanese transgender issues remains slight, and Mark Mc-Lelland (2000, 2002, 2004 and 2005) and Wim Lunsing (2003, 2005a and 2005b) have been invaluable as secondary sources on Japan's transgender identities. Fran Martin et al. comment on a US-centric approach in the developing global study of lesbian, gay and transgender identities, measuring non-Western queer communities against the yardstick of US and European developments. She notes that non-Western genders and sexualities are interpreted to 'imitate, appropriate and resist' Western paradigmatic queer identities, yet this cannot describe the complex process of hybridisation, whereby Western and non-Western cultures are mutually transformed (Martin et al. 2008: 3).

In the context of Japan, perhaps there is no better example of this than the direct wholesale import of Gender Identity Disorder (hereafter GID) and the transsexual identity from the US medical community into Japan between 1996 and 1998 against the backdrop of Japan's indigenous transgender identities, where many began to identify as being transsexual whilst simultaneously belonging to one of Japan's own identities such as *nyūhāfu* or *onabe* (see below). In this context, we could argue that the identity of an individual suffering from GID has merely been grafted onto Japan's own transgender identities, and that this US-created discourse has subsumed the wide variety of categories that actually exist in Japan.

In order to rediscover and understand the distinct experiences of Japan's transgender community, I have analysed the life stories contained in Harima Katsuki's book *Seidō itsusei shōgai: sanjū nin no kaminguauto* (Gender identity disorder: Thirty people come out, 2004), in which thirty transgender Japanese discuss their (trans-) gender identities. The book gives insight into how transgender lives in Japan are concretely affected by medical and legal barriers (such as in employment and family life), but also provides an opportunity to step outside of medical and legal discourse to discover how their identities may adhere to or challenge this homogenous discourse. In addition to the case studies in Harima's book, I will draw upon other Japanese-language primary sources such as newspaper articles and documentaries to access a multiplicity of transgender identities in Japan.

In Judith Butler's *Gender Trouble* (1990), 'drag' and 'performance' emerged as key words in Gender Studies. Butler argued that dressing and acting in 'drag' as the opposite sex parodied the notion of an original gender identity; if an individual can appropriate gendered appearance and behaviour not suited for their sex, they are exposing gender as a social construct. Judith Shapiro believes therefore that transgenderism belongs at 'the core of the sociological study of gender' (Shapiro 2005: 141). I hope that by using the transgender community as a point of departure, this dissertation will provide a valuable insight into various gender identities in Japan, and how and under what circumstances society, the law and medical establishment are willing to recognise transgender people's identities.

I will begin the discussion of Japan's post-war transgender identities with an account of the complications surrounding Sex Reassignment Surgery (SRS) that arose after the Blue Boy Trial. The next chapter will examine the appropriation of the (arguably Western) concept of transgenderism as GID and what effect this has had on Japan's transgender community. The following chapter examines the legislation and political discussion of transgender issues in Japan and how transgender lives remain complicated despite legislative progress. In the concluding chapter, I discuss various indigenous transgender identities in Japan that have been left out of medical and legal discourse after the appropriation of GID by Japan's medical community.

Nicola McDermott

POST-WAR TRANSGENDER LIVES

Transgender 'Boom'

Prior to the Second World War, Japan had a 'significant publications industry devoted to the discussion of sexuality, both healthy
and perverse' (McLelland 2004: 3). However, Japan's descent into
militarism in the 1930s halted these publications until the post-war
era of Allied occupation. McLelland (2005: 193) notes that post-
war print sources suggest an increase in both male and female
transgender practice in Japan, referring to the promulgation of
'gender deviant' behaviour as a 'boom'.

In the post-war years, knowledge of transsexualism began to
spread worldwide from the USA. In 1952, American Christine
Jorgensen (neé George William Jorgensen, Jr.) underwent a much
publicised series of sex reassignment operations in Denmark and
the United States. Her case was reported within the US-created
medical discourse of a person being 'born in the wrong body'. The
worldwide media was shocked and took an interest in Jorgensen
who then became a celebrity and transsexual spokesperson
(Shapiro 2005: 139).

Following the increased interest in transsexualism worldwide,
the visibility of transsexual individuals grew, including within the
entertainment districts of Japan. The Italian film *Europa di Notte*
(European Nights; directed by Alessandro Blasetti 1959) was released in Japan in 1961. The film featured European night-life,
including a French nightclub where the transgender dance troupe
'The Blue Boys' performed. They sparked the interest of both
underground and mainstream media in Japan and were invited to
perform as a cabaret act in bars in the *mizu shōbai* (lit. water trade;
Japanese night-life and sexual entertainment industry), first arriving
in Tokyo in 1963 (McLelland 2004: 8–9).

The Blue Boys were able to find a hospitable environment in
the *mizu shōbai*, as it had traditionally provided a safe space for

transgender identities. Japan has had virtually no sodomy or obscenity laws regarding homosexuality or gender deviant behaviour (Taniguchi 2006: 6), and cabaret clubs featuring trans-gender performers were never harassed or raided by police like they were in the USA during the 1960s (McLelland 2005: 195). Transgender people working in this industry have faced little problem with the law, and many performers went on to achieve mainstream stage careers, such as Miwa Akihiro and Carrousel Maki (McLelland 2004: 9). Although the worldwide interest in transgender identities stemmed from ostensibly Western models of people suffering from Gender Identity Disorder or GID, many in Japan were undergoing SRS (Sex Reassignment Surgery) and living as transgender outside of this medical discourse. McLelland notes that this surgery was performed on transgender people in Japan who were working in the *mizu shōbai* from 1951, a year before Jorgensen underwent her surgery (McLelland 2004: 15). As such a prominent employer of transgender individuals, the *mizu shōbai* has therefore been an important site for the development of various indigenous categories for transgender identities in Japan. Martin et al. (2008: 8) refer to an 'ongoing dominance of US-based research' which draws on 'an unquestioned assumption that the most interesting and important sites for queer analysis are to be found within the borders of the US nation state'.

The promulgation of the US-centric paradigm, whereby transgender identities are described under the category of 'trans-sexual', has led to many of these distinctly Japanese trans-gender experiences being largely ignored in global studies on transgender identities. For example, the 2006 volume *Transgender Rights* (Currah, Juang and Price Minter 2006) features only two articles on transgenderism outside of the US or Europe out of seventeen, both of which look at South American transgender rights. Moreover, a public forum debate sponsored by the University of Cambridge Centre for Gender Studies on 7 December 2010 in London called 'Transitioning Gender: The Challenges of Radical Technologies' ignored or at best seemed incognisant of the development of medical or legal rights outside of Europe.

Post-war Transgender Categories in the *Mizu Shōbai*

The clubs of the *mizu shōbai* often use their performers' transgenderism as a selling point for the mostly straight and gender-normative clientèle. For instance some male-to-female transgender acts in the 1980s were promoted as being more beautiful than 'real' women (Nakamura 2005: 9). Due to the marketing of transgenderism as a 'skill' or performance, McLelland (2005: 196) makes a distinction between semi-professional, professional and amateur transgender lives. The latter category includes those who attend cross-dressing clubs in their spare time where they have access to make-up and women's clothes such as at the Elisabeth Club in Kanda, Tokyo (Mitsuhashi 2007: 298–9). For those who derive their livelihood from the *mizu shōbai*, several categories have developed.

One of the most recognisable is the *okama,* a slang term for buttocks that literally means 'rice cooking pot' (McLelland 2004: 5). It is often translated into English as the equivalent of '[drag] queen', though Lunsing (2005b) notes it can also be used to refer to effeminate gay men. The *okama* is a hyper-feminine figure of fun who performs dance routines and provides humour for customers in the *mizu shōbai.* Much like drag queens in the West, they play up to exaggerated stereotypical feminine traits using flowery language and movements as well as elaborate hair and make-up to the point of over-performing their gender role. They are often portrayed as unable to 'pass' as genuine females because of this obvious distinction (McLelland 2002: 48).

Another category is *nyūhāfu* (newhalf), referring to non-normatively gendered biological males who work in the *mizu shōbai.* The term was invented by a transgender mama of an Osaka club ('I am half man and woman, so I'm a newhalf') and gained currency when it was propagated by newspapers in the early 1980s to describe famous transgender people (McLelland 2005: 198). Within the category are a wide range of bodies and identities and people in various stages of transitioning physically; some prefer the use of hormone injections alone to create feminine features, some have breast implants and some have not undergone any medical treatment at all. The majority do not define as the opposite sex, but as a mixture of both male and female (McLelland 2002: 168–9).

Female-to-male transgender identities in the *mizu shōbai* are not as common as male-to-female. The term *onabe* (also literally 'pot') has emerged as a prominent category to describe the non-normatively gendered biological females who work in the *mizu shōbai* host bars. In this capacity, they are 'special boyfriends' for the female customers for the duration of their visit to the bar. In return, the customers pay a small fee for entrance and are encouraged to buy expensive drinks. Although McLelland's research is important for understanding many of the male-to-female transgender categories, he does not offer as much information about female-to-male categories, citing lack of resources (2004: 16). However, in 1995 three *onabe* who worked at the New Marilyn Club in Tokyo (named Gaish, Tatsu and Kazuki) were interviewed extensively for Kim Longinotto's documentary *Shinjuku Boys,* filling in some of the gaps in knowledge and understanding of female-to-male categories.

Sharon Chalmers (2002: 31) attributes the lack of knowledge or research about female-to-male transgenderism in Japan to 'the androcentrism of most heterosexual social science disciplines'. Where they are included, Chalmers argues that researchers tend to 'add woman and stir'. This tendency to subsume female-to-male categories under male-to-female categories ignores how experiences differ between even normatively gendered men and women in Japan. This androcentrism and lack of knowledge about female-to-male categories is also reflected in the Japanese media, which has historically taken more interest in male-to-female categories in the *mizu shōbai,* though they are portrayed in a sensationalistic light.

Judith Halberstam (1998: 239) weighs in on the debate on the invisibility of female-to-male transgenders by arguing in her discussion of female masculinity that women who take on masculine dress and behaviour exhibit a much more downplayed version of 'drag'. They are therefore more convincing as 'real' men, which reduces the sensationalistic aspect of transgenderism that gender-normative people visiting the bars of the *mizu shōbai* may desire.

One example of the post-war 'boom' of interest in transgender people is 'Roppongi Girl' Matsubara Rumiko who, hiding her biological status as a man, entered and won a beauty promotion staged by businesses in Roppongi (a district in Tokyo famous for its night-life) to become the cover girl for a campaign promoting the area's bars in 1981. Once it was revealed that she was biologically male, she was quickly elevated to idol status, appearing in men's magazines (McLelland 2005: 198). The popularity Matsubara received as a direct consequence of her transgenderism is an example of the fascination the Japanese media has held for cross-dressing and transgender people within the entertainment industry. This interest was also reflected in Japanese women's magazines, which reported widely on SRS in the entertainment world in the 1980s.

We can see that since the 1960s the media had been reporting on transgenderism within the context of the entertainment world, and the Blue Boy performers became a frame of reference for transgenderism in Japan. So when a Japanese physician was arrested and tried in Tokyo for performing SRS on three biological males in 1970, the media reported it widely, coining it 'The Blue Boy Trial' (*burū bōi saiban*) (McLelland 2004: 9).

The Blue Boy Trial and the Eugenics Protection Law 1948

In 1970, an unnamed surgeon was imprisoned after being found guilty under Article 28 of the 1948 Eugenics Protection Law (*yūsei*

hogo hō) at Tokyo district court. He had removed the genitals of
three biological men as part of SRS (McLelland 2005: 206). Article
28 of the Eugenics Protection Law stated: 'No one shall, without
cause, perform an operation or an x-ray for the purpose of
rendering reproduction impossible, other than in cases provided for
in this act.' These cases were the possibility of passing on hereditary diseases or when a pregnancy could endanger the mother's
health. The law also stated that sterilising operations must be
carried out without removing the sex organs, so the physician was
charged under the full extent of the law and sentenced to up to one
year's penal servitude (Norgren 2001: 152).

The Eugenics Protection Law was created to legalise abortion
in the context of Japan's war-torn economy, as 'many feared that
the population growth [...] would render Japan incapable of economic recovery', and was also implemented in order to 'help
counteract hereditary disease' (Norgren 2001: 37). Article 4 mandated for the involuntary sterilisation of disabled citizens (Norgren
2001: 145–146) which provided a large source of contention for
disabled Japanese activists until its removal in 1996.

Thus, eugenics and the desire of the Japanese government to
exert control over its citizens' reproductive capacity provided the
context for the Blue Boy Trial rather than moral, religious or social
outrage about transgenderism. There was no penalty for the three
transgendered females, and it was not they, but the physician who
was on trial for violation of Japanese law.

Taniguchi notes that re-investigations after the initial trial by
legal journals such as *Bessatsu Juristo* 33 (1971) suggest that the
weight of the charges were brought because the physician acted for
his own commercial interest and he did not prove the surgery was
medically necessary as mandated in the act stated above (Taniguchi
2006: note 22). The biological males were identified in the case as
danshō, male-to-female cross-dressing prostitutes (Nakamura 2008:
8). Their desire for SRS was perhaps more tied up with the
demands of the sex industry than their gender identity, and so the
judges in this trial did not see the surgery as appropriate medical

treatment that justified the removal of the sex organs (McLelland 2002: 171).

As stated, the Japanese media had an interest in trans-genderism and SRS, so the media ensured that the trial was well reported and disseminated information about the severe reper-cussions the surgeon faced. This information reached physicians, who were made aware of the consequences of performing SRS, and thus fear of punishment drove them to halt performing the surgery for almost thirty years.

The case was pivotal in the history of medical treatment for transgender people in Japan, creating serious consequences for those who wished to access medical means of transitioning gender.

Hiatus in Legal Sex Reassignment Surgery in Japan

With this trial serving as a legal precedent, Japanese physicians were afraid to perform SRS, administer hormones or give advice to transgender people seeking medical treatment (McLelland 2005: 193). Many had to find other ways to change their bodies. In one tragic case in the 1960s, Nanjō Masami, a bar manager in Osaka, cut off her penis with a Japanese sword after an affair with a man who could not accept her biological sex. Although she survived after being found and eventually left Osaka with a male partner, her self-castration is an example of the lengths some felt they had to go to after the Blue Boy Trial (McLelland 2005: 197). Japanese who desired SRS had to go abroad to have the surgery, to places such as Thailand, America or Morocco.[16] Torai Masae, a prominent activist and author on transgender issues, underwent surgery in America in 1989, having saved money since high school to afford travel and medical costs (Harima 2004: 124). Many others could

---

[16] Interestingly, many Muslim countries such as Morocco and Iran advocate SRS to avoid same-sex relationships or unusually effeminate behaviour in men. See http: //news.bbc.co.uk/1/hi/7259057.stm (accessed 1 November 2012) for further discussion.

not afford this or had no access to relevant information. In the early 1990s, after the birth of the world wide web, transgender people could use bulletin board systems to share the contact details of the few doctors in Japan who were willing to remove the testes (McLelland 2005: 205), and hormones were also available on the black market (Mackie 2002: 216).

Still, Torai found that when he returned to Japan, many transgender people wanted information on SRS, so he started up *FTM Nippon* (Female-to-male Japan) in 1994, a magazine to share this information, as well as details of films or magazines that touched upon transgender issues (Harima 2004: 126–127). The desperation some Japanese transgender people felt in the absence of legal SRS and the interest in accessing medical treatment abroad demonstrates that there was a demand for SRS in Japan, and that the Blue Boy Trial had a detrimental effect on many transgender people's lives.

Nicola McDermott

THE IMPORT OF TRANSSEXUALISM INTO JAPAN

The Emergence of 'Gender Identity Disorder'

During the thirty-year period between 1970 and 1996, when the Japanese medical community was reluctant to discuss treatment for transgender people, physicians in the United States were instrumental in creating transsexualism as a diagnostic category. Harry Benjamin (1885–1986), an American endocrinologist, began to see patients in the 1950s and became a prolific writer on the subject of the newly discovered 'transsexualism'. He authored for instance *The Transsexual Phenomenon* (1966), in which he described transgender people as suffering from Gender Identity Disorder (GID). A popular discourse of people 'born in the wrong body' developed, and hormone replacement treatment (HRT) and Sex Reassignment Surgery (SRS) emerged as appropriate treatments.

Butler has argued that this diagnosis stigmatises individuals who have not properly embodied gender norms as 'ill, sick, wrong, out of order', rather than accepting their identity as 'what ought to be understood as one among many human possibilities of determining one's gender for oneself' (Butler 2004: 275). The diagnosis marks transsexuals as aberrations of the 'natural' relationship between sex and gender; the problem lies within the individual, rather than within a system that rigidly assigns people to one side of the gender binary. Rather than questioning the binary, the transsexual is marked as problematic and in need of correction. The assumption that they will desire surgery to achieve the 'right' genitals for their gender identity re-asserts anatomical sex as the basis for gender assignment. The creation of this model for gender-deviant behaviour has been described by Peter Conrad (1992: 210–213) as 'medicalisation', a process by which medical terminology comes to describe more and more parts of everyday life, in particular deviant behaviours. Within this process, frameworks to diagnose and treat behaviours which deviate from the mainstream are developed by the medical profession. In the same vein, beginning in the USA during the 1960s, non-normative gender identities have been placed under medical dominion. Due to increased faith in science and the prestige and power of the medical profession, the US medical community was successful in exporting the guidelines for diagnosis of GID to Europe, which then gained currency and widespread acceptance. In 1996 this widespread acceptance would then enable the Japanese medical community to present GID as a legitimate medical disorder in order to reverse the ban on reassignment treatment.

Although the diagnosis of GID pathologises transgender individuals, the prestige of the medical profession has led to transgender people now being recognised as having a legitimate medical condition that requires treatment. Butler (2004: 77) argues that many transgender people and physicians view the diagnosis as essential to justify serious surgery that involves removal of the sex organs. As we saw in the Blue Boy Trial, the Eugenics Protection Law forbade such surgery if it was not medically necessary. As the three transgenders who had received the surgery were *danshō* (male prostitute) who most likely treated the surgery as elective, the judges at Tokyo High Court could not find a medical disorder in the case that justified the surgery. In this context, now that the Japanese medical establishment had imported the model of transsexualism as a medical disorder that required treatment, this could help push towards resumption of legal SRS in Japan.

The Resumption of Legal Sex Reassignment Surgery

Although during the hiatus from 1970 to 1998 hormones could be bought on the black market and SRS was carried out illegally by some physicians, many transgender people in Japan still desired legalised SRS.

In 1996, the Eugenics Protection Law was replaced with the Protection of the Maternal Body Law (*botai hogo hō*). Vera Mackie suggests that this replacement and the removal of Article 28 were a precondition for the resumption of the surgery (Mackie 2002: 216). However, Article 28 remains as Article 9 in the same wording as part of the Protection of the Maternal Body Law. The cases in which sterilisation operations could be carried out had not been expanded, and proof that they were medically necessary, rather than elective, was still required. Therefore, the acceptance of GID as a legitimate disorder which required treatment by the Japanese medical establishment in 1996, rather than a change to the law, was the real reason for resumption of SRS.

The major change to the law was the removal of eugenic content. 'Eugenic operations' were renamed 'sterilisation operations' and Article 1 no longer described the law's purpose as 'prevent[ing] the birth of eugenically inferior offspring' (Norgren 2001: 155). Article 4, which mandated for the involuntary sterilisation of the handicapped, was not only removed, its inclusion within the original law provided the impetus for the law's revision in 1996.

The impetus came from left-wing feminist groups and handicapped rights groups in the 1990s. Unable to attract attention to their cause within Japan, these groups generated foreign pressure on the Japanese government at the 1995 Women's Conference in Beijing by drawing foreign delegates' attention to the 'Nazi-style mass sterilisation of those the state deemed unfit' (Norgren 2001: 79). Though the aims of this campaign were twofold, to remove the eugenic content and promote women's reproductive rights, only the handicapped activists' aims were achieved and abortion was not made available on demand (that is, performed on a woman solely at her own request, rather than only in health emergencies or for socio-economic reasons).

In the same year, a female-to-male transgendered person approached an unnamed surgeon from Saitama Medical School in Saitama prefecture requesting SRS, as this surgeon was skilled in reconstructing genitals of male patients involved in road traffic accidents (Lunsing 2003: 28). He asked the surgeon personally to perform surgery constructing a penis for him. The surgeon was sufficiently moved by his request to apply to Saitama Medical School's ethics committee for permission. Torai comments that it was this 'one patient who opened the door' for legal SRS in Japan (Harima 2004: 127). The ethics committee commissioned a report on GID and SRS from its medical team, which acknowledged that the disorder existed and that SRS was a medically justifiable activity (Takamatsu et al. 2001). The ethics committee requested guidelines for diagnosis, and physicians at the hospital drew these directly from guidelines by The Harry Benjamin International Gender Dysphoria Association (now named the World Professional Association for Transgender Health), publishing them in 1997. The first legal SRS in Japan was female-to-male and took place at Saitama Medical School in October 1998. There was no public criticism and the surgery was positively reported in mainstream Japanese media (Takamatsu et al. 2001).

SRS in Japan could resume once the available diagnosis of GID could prove such surgery to be medically justified, since the wording of the Protection of the Maternal Body Law required the Japanese medical community to accept transsexualism as a medical disorder. Whereas prior to the hiatus, the surgery was used by performers in the *mizu shōbai* to create more commercially viable female or male bodies for their line of work, after the resumption in 1998, the surgery could be performed only on those who fit the guidelines for diagnosing GID, which had been appropriated in their entirety from the US medical community. The credence and respect given to these guidelines in Japan post-1998 has meant that Japanese media and society have appropriated the hegemonic model of transsexualism, and some in the transgender community have internalised this model, marginalising Japan's indigenous transgender identities.

Nicola McDermott

Guidelines for Diagnosing Gender Identity Disorder

Following the resumption of legal SRS, the guidelines require that potential patients must prove that they are appropriate candidates for the surgery by convincing doctors that their change of gender identity is legitimate. Medical practitioners have posited themselves as 'gatekeepers' (*monban*) who control access to technologies for gender transition (Ishida 2002, quoted in McLelland 2004: 20). The decision is based on how much the patient is seen to fit into the guidelines, rather than the transsexual's desire for surgery alone.

According to the Japanese Society of Psychiatry and Neurology's third edition of guidelines for diagnosing and treating GID (*Seidō itsusei shōgai ni kan suru shindan to chiryō no gaidorain* 2006), patients must have experienced their current gender identity since childhood and feel distress about their body, whilst desiring SRS to achieve the body of the opposite sex.

These guidelines do not explicitly explore what is considered 'masculine' or what is 'feminine' and are vague enough for the diagnostician to decide what these gender norms are and whether a patient embodies them. According to the OECD (Organisation for Economic Co-operation and Development, Health Data 2002), in 1998, just 14.3 percent of doctors in the Japanese medical profession were female (compared to an average of 32.2 percent of the economically developed countries, and Finland's 50.7 percent). Thus, in the diagnosis process, 'male' and 'female' gender norms are decided by and large by male doctors and seen through a male gaze.

As discussed, the creation of transsexualism as a 'disorder' legitimises (anatomical) sex as the basis for gender identity. In addition to this normative view of gender assignment, the guidelines for diagnosis also reinforce conservative views of gender identity.

Gender Conservatism

Shapiro has argued that transgender people work at establishing their credentials as men or women in a relatively self-conscious way in order to pass as the opposite sex, so there is inevitably a degree of conservatism in their presentations of appropriate gender roles. She establishes that this 'gender conservatism is encouraged and re-enforced by the medical establishment on which they are dependent for therapy' (Shapiro 2005: 141). Butler argues that the main aim of the diagnosis is to ask if the patient is 'able to integrate into an established social world characterised by large-scale conformity to accepted gender norms' (Butler 2004: 281). Therefore transgender people who desire medical treatment are encouraged to present their gender somewhat stereotypically.

Udagawa Hiroki, a twenty-four-year old female-to-male transgender, is one example. He believes he exhibited male traits during childhood despite being raised as a girl. He recalls playing football and video-games with boys at school and hated wearing skirts. His mother insisted 'boys should be boys and girls should be girls', so it was only after his mother died that he felt able to cut his hair, wear trousers and eventually to begin living as male after graduating from high school (Harima 2004: 10–17).

Examining the guidelines for diagnosing GID, it is clear that this will be the sort of childhood story diagnosticians wish to hear from their 'patients'. For instance, the guidelines suggest that a male-to-female transgender may have adopted the 'mother' role playing 'house' during childhood (Meyer III 2001: 5), a notion which re-enforces gender stereotypes. Non-transgender people may have also engaged in activities stereotypically unsuited to their gender during childhood. Yet the diagnosis process, which is the hurdle to medical treatment for transgender people, encourages them to view their behaviour through a gendered lens and emphasise the childhood behaviour that is explicitly ascribed to the other gender.

Sexual Orientation

Another example of transgender people interpreting non-conformity to gender stereotypes as examples of their GID would be their views on sexual orientation. Takeru, who is a female-to-male transsexual from Saitama, Tokyo, describes the realisation that he was attracted to women as the first time he realised he was transgender; 'I thought, she's cute. That was the first time I realised that I thought like a man' (Harima 2004: 60). His opinion is that being attracted to females is a masculine trait and as such, he interprets the moment he realised he was sexually attracted to women to be the moment he realised that he wanted to become a man. This conflation of gender identity with sexual orientation effectively understands homosexuality as 'gender inversion'. Therefore, the diagnosis of GID presumes heterosexual desire and homosexuality is considered improper gendered behaviour (Butler 2004: 277).

By contrast, Gotō Misa is a male-to-female transsexual who is attracted to women and recognises that her gender identity and sexual orientation exist separately from one another; 'I'm attracted to women; I want to be a woman, but I like women. Sexuality is a different matter' (Harima 2004: 166). If the diagnosis presupposes heterosexuality as an important factor in gender identity, perhaps those who experience a lesbian identity or gay male identity may encounter more difficulties in convincing the diagnostician of the validity of their wishes relating to their gender identity.

Gender Differences and Sex Differences

The guidelines also place emphasis on the sense of disunity a patient will feel between their gender identity and their body, which will make them desire hormone replacement treatment and SRS to 'correct' this. Many of the interviewees recall puberty to be a difficult time when biological differences became more pronounced, feeling anguish towards a deepening voice and growing facial hair in the case of males, and development of breasts and menstruation for females. The guidelines encourage the doctor to interpret the distress a patient may feel about their body as proof of a direct link between male bodies and male identities, and female bodies and female identities. This idea of a coherent gender identity relating to the body re-establishes sexual difference as the basis for gender difference. For example, Tatsu, a female-to-male trans-gender person undergoing Hormone Replacement Therapy (HRT), is interviewed and asked questions about his realisation that he identified as male. He recalls the onset of menstruation as being a reminder that he was biologically female (*Shinjuku Boys* 1995).

However the guidelines do not ask whether it is the cultural meaning placed on such sex differences that create the distress in some patients. Halberstam argues that 'as soon as puberty begins, the full force of gender conformity descends onto the girl' (Halberstam 1998: 6) and the same can be said of boys. Through the deployment of the sex/gender binary where gender identity is assigned based upon biological and anatomical sex, the mani-festation of sex differences represents culturally the expectation that someone will conform to their assigned gender roles. Female bodies and biological functions are interpreted as 'woman' and the same is true for male bodies and functions which signal 'man'. Therefore the distress a transgender person may feel about sex differences and a desire to change them are interpreted by the guidelines as evidence that gender identity and biological sex are inextricably linked, whilst ignoring the cultural meaning that may be causing the distress.

However, not all transgender people wish to undergo full SRS. Yamauchi Toshio, a psychiatrist at Saitama Medical School states that less than 10 percent of those seeking medical treatment at their gender clinic wants to completely transform their bodies through surgery (Matsubara 20 June 2001).

Resistance to the Guidelines for GID

Although the import of a medical model from the USA has led to the availability of legal SRS, many members of Japan's transgender community resent having to conform to the guidelines for GID in order to receive medical treatment. Gotō Misa actively chose to acquire hormones and have SRS illegally. Her reason for avoiding institutionalised gender transition is that she does not wish to participate in a process that expects gender conformity and the stereotypical life histories the diagnosticians expect (Harima 2004: 168–169).

Others do not wish to receive medical treatment if their gender identity is considered a 'disorder'. Mitsuhashi Junko is a legal male who lives part-time as female and primarily identifies as a woman:

> I felt a considerable distaste for the idea that my proud lifestyle as a cross-dresser should be medicalised as some kind of 'disability' in need of cure by an institution. Therefore, even now, I have not done anything to transform my body biologically into that of a woman. (Mitsuhashi 2007: 309)

Despite considering medical intervention in order to create a more feminine body, Mitsuhashi decided against it *because* of the guidelines for GID. As she lives only part-time as a female, she would not fit into the guidelines which establish people as permanently on either side of the gender binary. Clearly, many in Japan's transgender community experience gender identities that are not reducible to the paradigmatic model of transsexualism. As some people's desire for SRS stems from commercial requirements of their jobs in the *mizu shōbai,* they do not fit into the medically sanctioned model for (trans)gender identities (McLelland 2004: 171). However, many of those interviewed by Harima (2004) identified themselves as suffering from GID or being transsexual, even if they did not fit properly into the guidelines, whilst also identifying themselves as *nyūhāfu.* This is an example of the mutual transformation and hybridisation of queer identities of which Martin et al. have spoken (Martin et al. 2008: 6). These examples of non-conformity with the medical model of GID do not only exist in Japan. Although the discourse has been accepted by many governments and medical establishments, transgender identities such as the *hijra* of India (Reddy 2010) or the *fa'afafine* of Samoa (Worth 2008), resist the proliferation of such homogenising discourses.

Conclusions

Since the proliferation of the World Wide Web and an increase in the amount of literature on this medical model, those who wish to access legal medical treatment can learn how to successfully convince diagnosticians of their eligibility for surgery. Therefore they may be willing participants as much as they are victims of the diagnosis process. Whilst their participation is understandable, Butler (2004: 281) worries that it may be used to strengthen the validity of a diagnosis which institutionalises conservative gender norms in a hegemonic model of non-normative gender identity.

Accompanying these developments, the Japanese mainstream media once more has taken an interest in transgender identities. Post-1998 they picked up this reductive and hegemonic model and began to discuss transgenderism within this context. However, this also meant that the media was discussing their situation with moral seriousness (McLelland, 2005: 194), in contrast to the sensationalism that was previously present. Now that within the Japanese medical community the stigma that surrounded performing SRS had been lifted, transgender people had established a level of respectability and could use the media's serious treatment of their identities to turn attention towards the legal and political issues they faced.

LEGAL AND POLITICAL ISSUES FACING TRANSGENDER PEOPLE

Violence towards and Harassment of Transgender People in Japan

Violence towards and harassment of LGBT (Lesbian, gay, bisexual and transgender) people often dominate discourse on transgender rights in Anglophone and Western European countries. Such violence and harassment occur with sufficient frequency that 85 countries from every world region signed an initiative to end these crimes at the UN Human Rights council at Geneva in March 2011 (*Herald Sun* 23 March 2011). In a recent instance of LGBT-motivated violence, male-to-female transgender Chrissy Lee Polis, 22, was attacked on 18 April 2011 by two women when trying to use the ladies' toilet in a branch of McDonald's in Baltimore, USA. A member of staff filmed the attack and can be heard laughing off camera (CNN 26 April 2011). This violent reaction towards transgender people is symptomatic of a prevalent and aggressive attitude holding that those who live outside of society's set gender and sexual norms must be forced to conform. Butler describes this attitude, which often translates into violence, as 'an attempt to show that this deviant behaviour is unthinkable, impermissible and will not go unpunished so as to preserve the order of the gender binary' (Butler 2004: 34–5). It is difficult to find a similar violent narrative for Japan. In this respect, Japan appears much more tolerant of non-normative gender identities than Western countries, where violence can often be a major threat to transgender people.

Scholars researching Japanese transgender lives often leave violence out of the discourse. In his discussion of LGBT rights in Japan, Lunsing devotes just one sentence to the subject, declaring it 'uncommon' and claiming that transgender people in Japan can live their lives openly without the problem of violence (Lunsing 2005a: 147). Significantly, in the interviews Harima conducted with transgender Japanese (2004), first-hand experience of violence or harassment is not mentioned.

However, after she announced her plan to run for a seat in Setagaya assembly on a political platform that promoted rights for transgender citizens and other minority groups, Kamikawa Aya (herself transgender) faced harassment in the form of defamatory posters in her home ward of Setagaya, as well as hate mail. The case could not be properly investigated, as Japanese law does not recognise harassment against people based upon their gender identity (*GayJapanNews* 2009: 3–4). The lack of antidiscrimination laws in Japan to protect LGBT citizens leaves no platform from which to investigate harassment or violence motivated by someone's (trans)gender identity, and therefore there is no frame of reference within Japanese law to register such acts as 'hate' crimes. Thus it may seem questionable that in the absence of official statistics, scholars are so ready to dismiss violence against transgender people as 'uncommon'. On the other hand, we cannot expect that the level of harassment Kamikawa faced is true for every transgender person in Japan. Many politicians may have found themselves the subject of defamatory campaigns, and the posters put up in Setagaya were removed by police immediately. The slogans were written from a Christian perspective (*GayJapanNews* 2009: 4), and as Christianity is not a dominant religion in Japan, it is likely that objections to Kamikawa's candidacy were only representative of a small group of citizens. Furthermore, Kamikawa won her seat in one of the richest and most conservative areas of Tokyo (Taniguchi 2006: note 28) and was placed sixth out of 72 candidates in April 2003 (*Japan Times* 3 May 2003). Her platform was explicitly in favour of transgender rights, and she remains in office (personal website http://ah-yeah.com), so it is clear that the campaign against her does not represent a mainstream view on transgenderism in Japan.

If we are to take Butler's argument that violence against transgender and LGB individuals is an attempt to enforce conformity to society's gender norms, the lack of a violent narrative for transgender people may point towards a tolerance in Japanese society that is perhaps not as widespread in many Western societies. However, this does not mean that transgender lives in Japan are not complicated by their gender identities.

To be sure, the main problems those interviewed by Harima (2004) reported were lack of legal recognition of their gender identity, lack of recognition from family and friends, difficulties finding work and the inability to marry their partners legally. Thus we can see that Japanese society and law still operates in such a way that fundamental parts of transgender people's lives are disadvantaged. One major problem is posed by the *koseki seido,* the administrative household registration system. This system registers Japanese citizens under their sex at birth, and, until 2004, their registered sex could not be changed.

The *koseki seido* and Problems for Transgender Citizens

The family registry, or *koseki seido*, is the Japanese system for recording the details of citizens as a member of a household under the head of the family. It records details such as births, marriages and deaths within the household and is the primary way to establish one's identity and to interact with the state (McLelland 2005: 207).

A citizen's gender on the *koseki* is restricted to one of two categories (male or female) and is recorded based upon anatomical sex (genital appearance) at birth. Yet in court proceedings, judges have previously decided gender is determined by chromosomal sex. In 1979, an individual who had undergone male-to-female SRS (presumably abroad as the surgery was still illegal) applied to change her gender on the *koseki* at Nagoya High Court, but was rejected on the premise that she was still male according to her chromosomes (Taniguchi 2006: 13). This is an inconsistent argument; anatomical sex provides the sole criterion for gender assignment at birth, but despite the plaintiff acquiring the correct genitals to be registered as female, the judge in this case decided that this aspect was trumped by chromosomal sex in an attempt to preserve sex at birth as the basis for gender in legal records. This marks a biologically deterministic attitude towards assignment of gender in the *koseki*, serving as a legal precedent for other similar cases.

For transgendered people, the *koseki* presents a particular problem in that it does not reflect their gender identity. Whilst they may be able to employ different strategies to establish themselves socially as male or female, and medical technology can help some acquire a body they feel is more consistent with their gender identity, the *koseki* system enforces gender as based on physical, biological and chromosomal factors. The *koseki* can serve to invalidate their gender identity in a fundamental way. In Karl Jacob Krogness's discussion of what he terms '*koseki* consciousness', he argues that based on the administrative household unit one belongs to, a citizen will form a 'meaningful manifestation contributing to the individual construction of legal and social identity' and as such the *koseki* is much more than a legal document (Krogness 2011: 65, 88). The *koseki seido* is not always representative of social and familial life, nor is it representative of one's gender. Therefore where legal and political discourse in Western countries places emphasis on allowing transgender people to change their birth certificate, Japan's transgender community has campaigned to change the gender listed in the *koseki*.

Another problem posed by the *koseki* is that Japanese are registered according to their position and role in a household, such as wife, eldest daughter, second eldest brother etc. The *koseki* constructs them legally in these roles, even though these descriptions may not reflect their subjective sense of family (Krogness 2011: 65). This particularly applies in the case of transgender citizens who may, for example, conceive of themselves as eldest sister, not eldest brother. This also causes issues for transgender people who wish to change *koseki* gender and therefore their position in the family, as younger siblings would also require alterations to their position in the family *koseki*.

Due to the different uses of the *koseki* this one document poses a major issue in day-to-day life for transgender people whenever production of their *koseki* is required. The *koseki* is necessary for access to rights and entitlements guaranteed to citizens of Japan, such as the right to vote, work, marry, choice of domicile and entitlement to welfare provided by the state. It is required when claiming medical insurance, applying for a passport, starting a new job, renting a flat or getting a mortgage (McLelland 2005: 208). Many transgender individuals therefore try to avoid these situations. Maeda Kentarō, a 37-year-old graphic designer from Tokyo, who has been through SRS and now lives as a man, explains the problems he experiences:

> Even though I live as a man, according to the *koseki* I am a woman, so filling in health insurance forms and such, I am a woman. At the hospital reception window, they ask me 'is this really you?' and other such inconvenient and uncomfortable questions. (Harima 2004: 104–105)

Maeda's gender identity is brought into question whenever he produces his medical insurance card which states that he is legally female. As the gender listed on this card must match the gender on their *koseki*, the implications of the *koseki* clearly go beyond administrative issues, and can impact access to healthcare (Mackie 2002: 217). The confused hospital receptionist is processing a man who holds a female *koseki,* and has to ask questions to certify the validity of his documents. The questions are not only awkward for Maeda, but his ability to establish himself as a 'normal' male within social interactions is compromised. For this reason, Maeda says that other transgender citizens avoid receiving healthcare altogether (Harima 2004: 104), potentially creating or exacerbating health problems and compromising their right to welfare.

Mackie suggests that transgender citizens are more likely to opt for casual and part-time work (particularly in the entertainment sector), which do not require proof of citizenship or other kind of registration, marginalising them from full-time, permanent and better-paid careers (Mackie 2002: 217). For the same reasons, we can assume that transgender citizens will be disadvantaged when renting apartments or travelling with a passport. It is clear that being able to change the gender registered on the *koseki* would not only bring legal recognition of their gender identities, but would improve their living standards and access to welfare and basic rights as Japanese citizens.

Therefore in the early 2000s, political discourse surrounding transgender rights centred on campaigning for a law to allow for legal gender change on the *koseki*. Prior to 2004, changes to the *koseki* could only be made when 'mistakes' were found (Mc-Lelland 2005: 208).

One main purpose for the introduction of the *koseki* after the Meiji restoration (1868) was to register those in Japan as citizens of the new nation state so as to maintain social order (Krogness 2011: 66). Thus the legal recording of the sex binary has historically been considered integral to protecting social order, and allowing people to freely change their gender of the *koseki* was considered a potential threat to this stability. As we saw with the case at Nagoya High Court, legal institutions are eager to maintain assignment of gender based on normative conceptions of sex. In order to change the way transgendered individuals' sex was legally documented, it was imperative that transgender citizens began educating the public about the problems posed by the *koseki* to garner public support for their lobbying of the government.

Transgender Lobbying and Activism

In the 1990s, there was limited legal or political discourse in mainstream media about the issues faced by transgender and transsexual citizens due to their *koseki* gender. The entertainment district continued to be hospitable to transgender people, yet did not provide the context for the development of political activism in the early twenty-first century. 'Newhalf' websites, places on the internet where so-called *nyūhāfu* can meet each other, are usually run by the owners of cabaret clubs that feature transgender performers and exist mainly for the purpose of promoting their businesses and advertising their services (McLelland 2002: 171). Therefore, although there were (online) spaces within the entertainment district for transgender people to meet that could have had the potential to act as a central site for political activism for the transgender rights movement, many working in the industry were uninterested in the politicised nature of Western transgender movements, instead choosing to use these sites as social spaces. The industry is often described as removed from the serious tone of full-time work and other industries (Allison 1991). Therefore political emphasis on transgender rights did not really exist, and the impetus for political activism came from outside the entertainment district, from individuals who worked in more 'serious' industries, such as Torai Masae, who is a writer.

As mentioned, in the 2000s after the resumption of legal SRS, mainstream Japanese media began to frame transsexualism as a serious medical issue (McLelland 2005: 206). The media began to publish articles featuring details about the legal issues transgender people still faced despite the resumption of SRS. Creating a movement for legal gender change required a strong group of transgender activists to disseminate information about transgender rights in order to gain support from the non-transgender public. Torai led a group of six transgender plaintiffs on 24 May 2001 to the Tokyo Family Court to file for gender change on their respective *koseki* (*Japan Times* 6 May 2001). Their appeals were rejected. However, it seems Torai was aware that this would be the outcome of their appeals, especially considering the result of the previous appeal at Nagoya High Court. As he had spoken to the *Japan Times* earlier that month informing them of the date they were to make their appeals, it would appear that his true intention was to highlight the issues posed by the *koseki* to the transgender community, and to demonstrate the reluctance of the Family Court to rectify the problem. He also used the opportunity to provide general information about transgender people for the mainstream press. It is clear therefore that this was part of a larger campaign. Their rejected appeals successfully highlighted the legal issues faced by transgender citizens and ensured coverage by the respectable press.

Around the same time as information regarding the legal issues transgender people faced reached mainstream Japanese society, Kamikawa became Japan's first transsexual elected politician, winning a seat in the Setagaya assembly in April 2003. Her victory can be seen as an example of the increasing acceptance afforded to transgender people in Japan after media attention began focusing on the political and legal issues they faced. Kamikawa's *koseki* gender was not only known by her voters, as it was reported in the media, but she had explicitly stated that her motivation for campaigning for office in Setagaya was to effect change for transgender citizens as a member of the Diet. Other issues she campaigns for are the rights of other disadvantaged social minority groups, such as the homeless, single-parent families and disabled people (personal website, http://ah-yeah.com).

Despite the attention the mainstream Japanese media was paying towards transgender political issues, the Diet was ignoring many of their campaigns for legal rights. Prior to Kamikawa's election victory, she found that her attempts to schedule meetings with Diet members and law makers to discuss these campaigns all failed, and decided entering office would be the best way to generate discussion in the Diet (Matsubara 2 March 2003). When Kamikawa submitted her documents to register as an election candidate, she left the column for sex blank, as she was still legally male. Yet Setagaya's election administration committee officially accepted her bid to run for office as a female, the first person to run for assembly under a different gender to the one listed on their *koseki* (*Japan Times* 21 April 2003). This decision possibly shows understanding of her situation by the Japanese political system, although a more cynical interpretation would be that the election administration committee was trying to avoid a media fallout as her plans to run for assembly had already been widely and positively reported in the press. Still, even this interpretation demonstrates that public support for transgender people could influence political protocol in Japan by the early 2000s. By 2003, transgender people had successfully made their campaign known via the Japanese media and managed to move it into the Diet. The scene was set for the Diet members to begin drafting a law allowing legal gender change.

In February 2003, members of the Liberal Democratic Party (LDP) commissioned a study group into transgenderism, and they incorporated the results into the drafting of this law alongside members of the New Komeitō Party (Ishida 2008: 22). The bill passed the Diet unanimously in July 2003, and came into effect in July 2004 (Ishida 2008: 23–24). The political campaigns of Torai and other activists had come to fruition. However, the law has since been the focus of much debate amongst transgender and LGB communities (Taniguchi 2006: 16).

Legal Gender Change: the *Tokureihō*

The law allowing for legal gender change was titled the 'Special Act for the Treatment of the Gender of Individuals Suffering from GID' (*Seidō itsusei shōgaisha no seibetsu no toriatsukai no tokurei ni kan suru hōritsu,* hereafter *Tokureihō*[17]). The law listed five requirements that individuals must meet before their local Family Court would allow the alteration in the *koseki*:

Article 3, Clause 1: Five Necessary Conditions

1. Must be twenty years and older.

2. Cannot currently be married.

---

[17] In Japanese literature regarding this law, the title is most often shortened to *Tokureihō*.

3. Does not have any children.

4. Does not have reproductive glands and is unable to reproduce.

5. Has genitals with the approximate appearance of those of the opposite sex (*ta no seibetsu ni kakaru shintai no seiki*).

(Ishida 2008: 21)

A further requirement for the applicant is to present papers of their diagnosis of GID by at least two doctors ordained by the Ministry of Health, Labour and Welfare (listed in Article 2). Those who received medical treatment abroad or illegally in Japan would therefore have to contact Japanese doctors for a diagnosis before applying to change their *koseki* gender.

The strictness of these requirements has been the subject of much debate amongst the transgender and LGB community. Whilst many were pleased that there was now a law allowing legal gender change, the conditions outlined in the law have left many unable to alter their *koseki*.

The first requirement that only those twenty years and older of age could change their *koseki* has been the least controversial. Drafters of the bill decided that since only few transgender people under twenty years old were receiving medical treatment, it would not be long until they reached adult age and could change their *koseki* (Ishida 2008: 115).

The second and third requirements are perhaps the most problematic for the family lives of transgender people. The exclusion of married transgender people was made into law, as one of the drafters of the bill stated, to avoid same-sex marriage in Japan (Taniguchi 2006: 24). Those who wish to acquire the protections for their same-sex relationship, such as the right to make a decision in a medical emergency or inheritance rights, can acquire these through the adult adoption (*yōshien gumi*) system, with the older partner adopting the younger partner (Taniguchi 2006: 21, Maree 2004: 544). However, this does not eliminate legal ties to one's actual parents. The 'child' enters the *koseki* of the 'parent' and can receive sole inheritance rights in the case of death, but in the case of death of the 'child', their property can be distributed amongst all their existing family members. The partner registered as parent therefore receives fewer inheritance rights, so this system does not by any means give same-sex couples the same rights afforded by marriage, and many still desire the right to marry legally (Maree 2004: 544). The law-makers seem to have been worried that if someone presently married were to change gender on the *koseki*, not only would this mean two people of the same sex could be married, it would give activists a strong and legitimate platform to campaign for same-sex marriage.

According to a survey carried out by Ishida Hitoshi in 2003 for his study on GID and the law, at least 15.6 percent of transgender people surveyed were married (Ishida 2008: 48). If these people wish to change the gender on their *koseki,* they will have to dissolve the marriage regardless of whether they wish to do so, and those who identify as homosexual will lose the right to marry if they switch gender on the *koseki.* This regulation of individuals' right and choice to marry is therefore included in the law to preserve marriage as a heterosexual institution.

For the same purpose, those with children were excluded. This requirement was relaxed in 2007 to only exclude those with children under twenty years of age (Ishida 2008: 75). This stipulation seems to have been included in the law to prevent same-sex parenting and to keep the nuclear family hetero-centric. One of the concerns expressed by drafters of the bill was that if a child were to have a mother who became a father or a father who became a mother, 'for the child, that would create a situation which is psychologically and socially really difficult and harsh' (Ishida 2008: 24). However, this concern does not ask whether it is social attitudes that may cause 'difficult and harsh' situations for the child, nor does it question what sort of situation preventing a transgender parent from changing their *koseki* gender may create for the parent or child. For example, I have discussed how being unable to change *koseki* gender may marginalise transgender people from full-time, well-paid work. For the transgender who has a school-age child (or several), this stipulation may create a financial burden on the household if they are unable to bring in an adequate wage. Therefore, far from looking after the best interests of the child, this law may *create* a difficult situation for the family. Further, many of Harima's interviewees (2004) have children who watched their gender transition, such as Tōi Itsuki, a male-to-female transgender who has two children with her wife, to whom she remains married. The children are young and have actually 'accepted [her] gender transition naturally' and are yet to experience a 'difficult and harsh' situation relating to their parent's gender identity (Harima 2004: 146). Another of the law makers' worries was that young children would 'internalise' their parent's transgenderism (Ishida 2008: 122), although presumably this could happen without legal gender change. This attitude marks non-normative attitudes towards gender assignment as problematic and something that must be avoided. Therefore it seems that rather than affording transgender people respect and acknowledgement of their gender identity, the law is occupied with maintaining the hetero-sexual nuclear family.

The final two requirements make sterility and SRS manda-tory for those wishing to legally change gender. Masaki Masatani from Akita prefecture is a female-to-male transgender who is head of the organisation *Sei wa jinken ESTO,* (ESTO – sex[uality] is a human right), which campaigns for lesbian, gay and transgender rights in Japan. He does not wish to have full SRS, and so finds these requirements 'humanely and ethically unforgivable' (Harima 2004: 43). Undergoing such serious surgery should be the individual's choice rather than a legal requirement. As stated, less than 10 percent of those seeking medical treatment at Saitama gender clinic in 2001 expressed desire to completely transform their bodies through surgery. The law therefore undercuts the autonomy of transgender citizens in Japan, as those who wish for legal gender change may feel forced to undergo surgery to conform to the *Tokureihō*'s requirements. Yamanaka Michihisa, a female-to-male transgender aged twenty-four is one such person:

> In the future, I want to marry my girlfriend, but I can't because I can't change my sex on the *koseki*. I'm not sure whether or not to get sex reassignment surgery. There's the problem of the cost, and the surgery is a big and risky operation [...]. Why you can't change your gender without having surgery, I don't understand. So, obviously staying as I am, I can't get married ever. (Harima 2004: 23–24)

As Yamanaka is legally female until he undergoes SRS he cannot change his *koseki* and marry his girlfriend, and although he is unsure about having the surgery, he is still considering it so that he can get married. He has issues with the costs and the risk of serious surgery. SRS is not covered by health insurance policies in Japan (Ellis 2006), so the patient must pay for the full cost of the expensive surgery. Furthermore, Japan currently has only two major hospitals that offer SRS (one each in Kansai and in Saitama near Tokyo), so access is contingent on the patient's ability to pay and travel. Therefore one of the requirements on the *Tokureihō* not only undercuts a patient's free choice, but disadvantages those who do not have the funds, or live far away from a clinic.

The Japanese law's requirement for SRS re-establishes anatomical sex and the 'right' sex organs as the basis for gender assignment. In 1979 the transsexual who had undergone SRS was refused legal gender change by Nagoya High Court due to a belief that gender assignment would be based on chromosomal sex, whereas the 2003 law has established it will be decided by anatomical sex. Shapiro (2005: 147) believes whilst many desire the genitals of the opposite sex, there will be those who are 'simply conforming to their culture's requirement for gender assignment' and this law has done little to fundamentally change this by re-entrenching this cultural requirement in the law. Taking the requirements into account, it is unsurprising that the *Tokureihō* passed unanimously through the Diet when the conservative Liberal Democratic Party was in power.

Kamikawa and Torai both changed their gender on the *koseki* after the enactment of this law (*Urb* magazine 2003; Harima 2004: 127). Though Kamikawa retains her seat in the Setagaya assembly, with the two main activists for *koseki* gender change having their personal aims fulfilled, the ferocity of their fight for further alterations to the law has likely been diminished. Furthermore, the campaign gained support when there was no system for changing gender on the *koseki*. With the enactment of the *Tokureihō,* this platform has disappeared. Although the law is strict, the impetus to change it further will be mostly coming from transgender people themselves, and is not so much of an issue in the mainstream Japanese press.

Those who do not meet the requirements perhaps now face a bigger obstacle for legal gender change than before. After the enactment of the law in July 2004, 208 people successfully applied to have their *koseki* gender changed (Taniguchi 2006: 15). However, ten were rejected. By July 2007, 840 applications were accepted out of 871 (Ishida 2008: 24). These numbers do not include those who did not even bother to apply as they knew they would be rejected. Whilst the law has eased the lives of those who meet the requirements, those who do not meet them, still face obstacles in obtaining work and getting married. The existence of the *Tokureihō* poses a barrier to further discussion or expansion of the criteria for legal gender change.

Conclusion

The medical and legal discourse that I have discussed presents transgenderism as an aberration of the sex/gender binary which can be corrected through medical intervention. Since 1998 and the wholesale import of a US-made medical model for transgenderism, individuals have been able to undergo surgery and through the *Tokureihō*, re-enter society as a 'normal' member of the opposite sex. This is a hegemonic model which has overshadowed and marginalised much of Japan's transgender community, including those who do not conform to the sex-based requirements for gender assignment, or who do not wish to be placed on either side of the gender binary. These transgender identities have been pushed aside by the mainstream influential discourse in medicine, politics and the media, yet are perhaps a much more interesting and complex addition to the global discourse on transgender identities.

TRANSGENDER IDENTITIES BEYOND LEGAL AND MEDICAL DISCOURSE

Transgender in the Media

The media in Japan and transgenderism have had a long and varied relationship. Images of cross-dressing and transgender individuals have been widespread in both the mainstream and underground press, and are often interpreted to show an acceptance of subversive gender behaviour that is not present in Western media. Takeda Sachiko, a researcher on gender at Osaka University, comments that *nyūhāfu* who are 'more beautiful than supermodels [...] make the rounds of popular lifestyle and opinion talk shows [...]. It is as if the Japanese mass media has no taboo against cross-dressing' (Takeda 1999: 187). We have also seen how in the post-war years, the transgender Blue Boy dance troupe gained wide-spread acclaim and popularity in the media during their tour of Japan. However, this media attention is most often sensationalist, finding transgender people objects of fascination, which can further encourage differences between gender-normative and transgender people.

Although some *nyūhāfu* are shown by the media to be more beautiful than 'real' women, the Japanese media portrays some of them as figures of fun, such as the *okama*. The humour of the *okama* derives from presenting the *okama* as desperately trying to 'pass' as female but failing; humorous but 'ultimately sad and pathetic women *manqué*' (McLelland 2000: 49, 59). For example, Haruna Ai, a regular guest on daytime television shows (who actually refers to herself as a *nyūhāfu*) is subject to her non-transgender co-hosts pointing out her 'masculine' muscles and referring to her as Ken-chan, a common diminutive for her male birth name Kenji (*Haruna Ai ni nani o kiku?* 7 September 2010), thereby making sure the audience is aware that she is biologically male. By refusing to validate her gender identity, this portrays her as 'failing' to be a woman. Yet in the documentary *Judith Butler: Philosophical Encounters of the Third Kind* (Zajdermann 2007), Butler comments that 'gender is always a failure', for both transgender and non-transgender people, as no-one can fully embody all of society's gender norms. If the media presented the transgender as able to 'pass' by accepting them as ordinary women and men (as many transgender people surely would wish them to do so), it would reiterate Butler's argument that this would 'parod[y] the notion of an original gender identity' (Butler 1990: 140). Since the media does not present them as such, this underlines that they are unwilling to accept transgendered people's identities as genuine despite eagerly featuring them in magazines and on television. This presentation of transgender people not being 'real' men or women re-establishes the notion of a natural gender identity that stems from biological sex.

However, the media has portrayed female-to-male trans-genderism more seriously since they began reporting legal and political transgender issues, and therefore featured activists such as Torai (McLelland 2005: 207). Tokyo Broadcasting System asked Torai permission to include his story in an episode of the 2001 series of *Kinpachi Sensei* (Teacher Kimpachi) (Harima 2004: 128), a Japanese drama that has traditionally dealt with breaking down prejudice surrounding stigmatised social issues (Ellis 2006). The inclusion of Torai's story by a major broadcaster may be because female-to-male transgender political campaigners in particular were framed by the media as part of the normalising discourse of GID, a discourse which has gained currency due to its normalisation of transgender issues. The nature of this discourse enables access to medical treatment and legal gender recognition, and helps to promote acceptance and respect for transsexuals who desire to fit into the gender binary. However, it has left the notion of gender as a result of anatomical sex intact, and the assumed binary nature of gender unchallenged. This has created an (ostensibly Western-made) model for transgenderism that pushes aside Japan's indi-genous transgender categories. The media as well as medical community, legal institutions, and the Diet have unsurprisingly accepted the model of a patient who, as a normative representation of a man or woman, can simply be re-categorised as the opposite sex. They have chosen to overlook the transgender identities in Japan that pose radical challenges to the common assumption of a natural and fixed sex/gender binary.

Japan's Indigenous Transgender Identities

As established earlier, the *mizu shōbai* industry has offered trans-gender identities a hospitable environment in the post-war years, and due to the issues raised regarding the *koseki* and obtaining work, many transgender people prefer to seek work in this industry. McLelland notes that there are also those who actively seek work in this industry as it could offer not only employment but a site to fully develop their transgender identities (McLelland 2005: 193). The industry does not suit all, however, as some resent having to put on performances in the sexualised atmosphere of the clubs and bars.

Two of the identities supported within the *mizu shōbai* industry are *onabe* and *nyūhāfu*. People within these categories, which may best be described as occupational categories rather than identities, cannot really be said to want to live as only either male or female. They are in various stages of treatment; some *nyūhāfu* are using hormones to acquire more feminine features such as breast growth, some have breast implants and many express a desire to keep their male sex organs whilst maintaining a feminine aesthetic to their clothes and make up (McLelland 2002: 170). As many *nyūhāfu* are sex workers, they often keep their sex organs in order to please more clients, and their medical transition is tied up with the demands of the industry as much as with their personal desires. The same is true of the *onabe*. There are two rival *onabe* clubs in Tokyo; Apollo and The New Marilyn. At Apollo, taking male hormones is obligatory, so that the hosts develop facial hair and deeper voices, and over half of them have had mastectomies (Lunsing 2005b: 89). Most of the *onabe* working at The New Marilyn have not taken any steps towards medical treatment, and only a few take hormone injections (*Shinjuku Boys* 1995). The owners of the Apollo even use the fact that their hosts have undergone more medical treatment and so have more conventionally male-looking *onabe* as a selling point to their gender-normative clientèle (Lunsing 2005b: 90). That their desire to transition may stem from patrons' commercial desires contravenes the model of transgender people with GID who desire the surgery after being 'born in the wrong body'.

The various physical features of *onabe* and *nyūhāfu* signify that they occupy an intermediary status between the genders, and their identities reflect this. Even the term *nyūhāfu* (newhalf) describes a state of being half man, half woman. Misaki, webmistress of a *nyūhāfu* website describes herself as 'hav[ing] a female heart but being 10 percent male' and says 'Some may think I want to live as a woman, but I don't; I just want to live as myself'. Gaish, an *onabe,* says 'I don't particularly think of myself as a woman or a man, I'm just me' and describes himself as 'in-between' (*chūkan*) (*Shinjuku Boys* 1995). Another *onabe* interviewed for an episode of Jonathan Ross's *Japanorama* (*Ai to koi*, 26 March 2007) described himself as 'half man, half woman'. These identities therefore cannot be placed comfortably within the categories of male or female and so are not represented by the dominant discourse on transgenderism. As such these categories have been overlooked by the mainstream media which prefers to present transgender people within the dominant narrative of GID. This re-establishes the polarity of gender identity.

With the narrative of GID dominating mainstream discourse, the *mizu shōbai* seems to be the only industry where these identities can flourish. Therefore when McLelland says that some actively seek work in this industry, it seems likely that they are doing so because of the freedom it offers them to 'live as themselves', rather than perhaps a calling to perform in bars and clubs. Anne Allison, an anthropologist who studied the *mizu shōbai* in the 1980s, comments that the industry connotes 'fluidity – an occupation that one can float into and out of without the rigidity required by other forms of employment and a service that one can enjoy while being freed from duties and responsibilities that matter elsewhere' (Allison 1994: 33). Thus it is an industry separate from the serious-ness and certain responsibilities of jobs in which the majority of Japanese work. As such, *onabe* and *nyūhāfu* identities, which demonstrate the ability to live a life beyond or between the strict boundaries of the gender binary, only visibly exist in a non-mainstream space. Those who wish to live beyond the gender binary may feel the *mizu shōbai* is the only place they can make a living whilst enjoying their lifestyle. For instance, Toi Itsuki, a male-to-female high school teacher from Kyoto, used to see *nyūhāfu* on television; 'Whilst watching, I would think "Oh, I want to be like them." But I enjoyed my work as a teacher and could not throw that away' (Harima 2004: 141). For Toi, transgenderism seemed incompatible with an ordinary job as a high school teacher. Whilst living as a man, the overall impression he received was that conforming to his male gender role was necessary in order to continue work in a 'serious' industry. The sharp divide between the 'real world' and the *mizu shōbai* has therefore also created a sharp divide between transgender people and 'normal' men and women, yet for those who conform to the normalising discourse of transsexualism, there is an opportunity to change their *koseki* and enter mainstream Japanese society re-categorised as the opposite sex.

CONCLUSIONS

I have argued that the homogenisation of transgender identities into the medical model of transsexualism has subsumed and marginalised indigenous and complex transgender categories in Japan. Given that the diagnosis of Gender Identity Disorder re-establishes conservative gender norms as well as genitals as the basis for gender assignment, it is not surprising that the Japanese medical community, Diet and media have chosen to recognise trans-sexuality over indigenous transgender categories.

Therefore despite the resumption of legal sex reassignment surgery in 1998 and the enactment of a law allowing for legal gender change in the *koseki* in 2003/2004, those who do not fit into the transsexual paradigm of 'patient' find themselves unable to take advantage of medical and legal progress and are disadvantaged in various fundamental areas of their lives.

Perhaps medical and legal recognition of transsexualism are not an attempt to ameliorate transgendered lives or a benefit to those whose identities fall outside of the sex/gender binary. What really seems to be happening is a trade-off between the state and transgender citizens. Transgender people may receive legal rights, but only if they are complicit with a state-sanctioned normalising discourse. In effect, the Japanese government bribes transgender people with legal recognition, employment and marital rights, and in return, transgender people must admit to being wrong, out of order and sick, and slot themselves back into society as an 'accurate' representation of a heteronormative man or woman.

Individuals such as Mitsuhashi Junko present a radical challenge to the state's desire to place all its citizens within comfortable and coherent gendered categories. A biological male with a wife and children, she describes herself as a 'part-time male-to-female transgender' and lectures as a social historian at Chūō University as female. Her areas of interest include the history of transgender identities and cross-dressing in Japan (Mitsuhashi 2007: 295–296). She refuses to place herself on either side of the gender binary permanently, yet has established herself as a respected academic and author, studying Japan's distinct transgender and cross-dressing categories. Perhaps if the mass media more readily discussed individuals such as Mitsuhashi who cannot be comfortably described as 'transsexual', nor as either only 'male' or 'female', we would see more inclusion of Japan's own indigenous transgender identities. This may in turn lead to the discussion of identities which challenge the validity of the sex/gender binary and how they are deployed for transgendered people.

Nicola McDermott

REFERENCES

AFP News (3 December 2009): '*Japan Transsexual Queen Wants Her Country More Tolerant.*' http://www.google.com/hostednews/afp/article/ALeqM5jnK7ExzIExqQFKd4SnY8X1fvb90g (accessed 4 November 2012).

Allison, Anne (1994). *Nightwork. Sexuality, Pleasure, and Corporate Masculinity in a Tokyo Hostess Club.* Chicago: University of Chicago Press.

Benjamin, Harry (1966). *The Transsexual Phenomenon.* New York: Julian Press.

Butler, Judith (1990). *Gender Trouble: Feminism and the Subversion of Identity.* New York: Routledge.

Butler, Judith (2004). *Undoing Gender.* New York: Routledge.

Chalmers, Sharon (2002). *Emerging Lesbian Voices from Japan.* London: RoutledgeCurzon.

CNN (26 April 2011). 'Prosecutors Weigh Additional Charges in Maryland McDonald Attack'. http://articles.cnn.com/2011-04-25/justice/maryland.mcdonalds.beating_1_transgender-woman-baltimore-county-police-count-of-first-degree-assault?_s=PM:CRIME (accessed 4 November 2012).

Conrad, Peter (1992). 'Medicalisation and Social Control', *Annual Review of Sociology* 18, pp. 209–232.

Currah, Paisley, Richard Juang and Shannon Price Minter (2006 eds). *Transgender Rights.* Minneapolis: University of Minnesota Press.

Ellis, Justin (2006). 'I Want to be Myself: Perspectives on Japan's Transgender Community', *Kyoto Journal: Perspectives on Asia, 64 'Unbound: Gender in Asia'*, pp. 14–16.

GayJapanNews (2009). 'JAPAN: Discrimination against Lesbians, Bisexual Women and Transgender Persons: A Shadow Report', International Gay and Lesbian Human Rights Commission (IGLHRC). http://www2.ohchr.org/english/bodies/cedaw/docs/ngos/Japan_LBT_May09_japan_cedaw44.pdf (accessed 25 November 2012).

Halberstam, Judith (1998). *Female Masculinity.* Durham: Duke University Press.

Harima Katsuki (2004 ed.). *Seidō itsusei shōgai: Sanjū nin no kaminguauto* (Gender Identity Disorder: Thirty people come out). Tōkyō: Futabasha.

Herald Sun (23 March 2011). 'US Hails World Move to End Violence Against Gays'. http://www.heraldsun.com.au/news/ breaking-news/us-hails-world-move-to-end-violence-against- gays/story-e6frf7k6-1226026852281 (accessed 4 November 2012).

Ishida Hitoshi et al. (2008 ed.). *Seidō itsusei shōgai: Jendā, iryō, tokureihō* (Gender Identity Disorder: Gender, medical treatment and the *Special Act for the Treatment of the Gender of Individuals Suffering from Gender Identity Disorder*). Tōkyō: Ochanomizu Shobō.

Japan Times (6 June 2001). '*Transsexuals Set to File Civil Lawsuits: Battleground Moves as Six Aim to Record New Genders on Family Registers*'. http://www.japantimes.co.jp/ text/nn20010506a6.html (accessed 25 November 2012).

Japan Times (21 April 2003). '*Setagaya OKs Transsexual's Election Bid*'. http://www.japantimes.co.jp/text/nn200304- 21a5.html (accessed 25 November 2012).

Japan Times (3 May 2003). 'Transsexual Starts Work at Assembly'. http://www.japantimes.co.jp/text/nn20030503b6.html (accessed 25 November 2012).

Krogness, Karl Jacob (2011). 'The Ideal, the Deficient, and the Illogical Family. An Initial Typology of the Administrative Household Units', Richard Ronald and Allison Alexy (eds) *Home and Family in Japan. Continuity and Transformation.* New York: Routledge, pp. 65–90.

Lunsing, Wim (2003). 'What Masculinity? Transgender Practices Among Japanese "Men"', James Roberson and Suzuki Nobue (eds) *Men and Masculinities in Contemporary Japan. Dislocating the Salaryman Doxa.* London: RoutledgeCurzon, pp. 20–37.

Lunsing, Wim (2005a). 'LGBT Rights in Japan', *Peace Review: A Journal of Social Justice* 17, pp. 143–148.

Lunsing, Wim (2005a). 'The Politics of *okama* and *onabe*. Uses and Abuses of Terminology Regarding Homosexuality and Transgender', Mark McLelland and Romit Dasgupta (eds) *Genders, Transgenders and Sexualities in Japan.* New York: Routledge, pp. 81–95.

Mackie, Vera (2002). 'Embodiment, Citizenship and Social Policy in Contemporary Japan', Roger Goodman (ed.) *Family and Social Policy in Japan. Anthropological Approaches.* Cambridge: Cambridge University Press, pp. 200–233.

Maree, Claire (2004). 'Same Sex Partnerships in Japan: Bypasses and Other Alternatives', *Women's Studies* 33, pp. 541–549.

Martin, Fran et al. (2008). 'Introduction', Fran Martin et al. (eds) *AsiaPacifiQueer. Rethinking Genders and Sexualities.* Urbana, Il.: University of Illinois Press, pp. 1–27.

Matsubara Hiroshi (20 June 2001). 'Sex Change No Cure For Torment: Surgery an Option but Transsexuals Still Face Legal Walls', *Japan Times.* http://www.japantimes.co.jp/text/nn 20010620c1.html (accessed 25 November 2012).

Matsubara Hiroshi (2 March 2003). 'Transsexual Out to Change Family Registry Law'. *Japan Times.* http://www.japantimes. co.jp/text/nn20030302a7.html (accessed 25 November 2012).

Mitsuhashi Junko (2007). 'My Life as a "Woman"', Translated by Suganuma Katsuhiko. Mark McLelland, Suganuma Katsuhiko and James Welker (eds) *Queer Voices from Japan: First Person Narratives from Japan's Sexual Minorities.* Plymouth: Lexington Books, pp. 295–312.

McLelland, Mark (2000). *Male Homosexuality in Modern Japan: Cultural Myths and Social Practices.* London: Routledge.

McLelland, Mark (2002). 'The Newhalf Net: Japan's "Intermediate Sex"', *International Journal of Sexuality and Gender Studies* 7/ 2–3, pp. 163–175.

McLelland, Mark (2004). 'From the Stage to the Clinic: Changing Transgender Identities in Post-war Japan', *Japan Forum* 16/1, pp. 1–21.

McLelland, Mark (2005). *Queer Japan from the Pacific War to the Internet Age*. Maryland: Rowman and Littlefield.

Nakamura Mia (2005). *Kokoro ni wa seibetsu wa aru no ka? Seidō itsusei shōgai no yori yoi rikai to kea no tame ni* (Is there a gender difference in your heart? For understanding and care for Gender Identity Disorder). Tōkyō: Iryo-bunka-sha.

Nihon Seishin Shinkei Gakkai: Seidō Itsusei Shōgai ni Kansuru Iinkai (Japanese Society of Psychiatry and Neurology: Committee for Gender Identity Disorder) (2006). *Seidō itsusei shōgai ni kansuru shindan to chiryō* (Guidelines for diagnosing Gender Identity Disorder and treatment). Third edition. http://www.jspn.or.jp/ktj/ktj_k/gid_guideline/gid_ guideline_manuduction.pdf (accessed 15 November 2012).

Norgren, Tiana (2001). *Abortion Before Birth Control: The Politics of Reproduction in Post-war Japan*. Princeton: Princeton University Press.

Organisation for Economic Co-operation and Development, Health Data (2002): 'Female Doctors by Country.' http://www. nationmaster.com/graph/lab_fem_doc-labor-female-doctors (accessed 4 November 2012).

Reddy, Gayatri (2010). *With Respect to Sex: Negotiating Hijra Identity in South India*. Chicago: University of Chicago Press.

Shapiro, Judith (2005). 'Transsexualism: Reflections of the Persistence of Gender and the Mutability of Sex', Jennifer Robertson (ed.) *Same-sex Cultures and Sexualities*. Oxford: Blackwell, pp. 138–161.

Takamatsu Ako et al. (2001). 'Beginnings of Sex Reassignment Surgery in Japan', *International Journal of Transgenderism* 5/1. http://www.wpath.org/journal/www.iiav.nl/ezines/web/ IJT/97-03/numbers/symposion/ijtvo05no01_02.htm (accessed 4 November 2012)

Takeda Sachiko (1999). 'Menswear, Womenswear: Distinctive Features of the Japanese Sartorial System', Translated by Sarah Teasley. Wakita Haruko, Anne Bouchy and Ueno

Chizuko (eds) *Gender and Japanese History* Vol. 1*: Religion and Customs/the Body and Sexuality.* Osaka: Osaka University Press, pp. 187–211.

Taniguchi Hiroyuki (2006). 'The Legal Situation Facing Sexual Minorities in Japan', *Intersections: Gender, History and Culture in the Asian Context* 12. http://intersections.anu. edu.au/issue12/taniguchi.html (accessed 25 November 2012).

Urb Magazine (2003). *'Watashi wa, sanjū sai kara, josei toshite iki hajimemashita'* (Age 30, I started living as a woman). http://ah-yeah.com/images/press/0900urb.jpg (accessed 4 November 2012).

Meyer, Walter III (Chairperson) (2001). Harry Benjamin's International Gender Dysphoria Association's Standards of Care, sixth version, The World Professional Association for Transgender Health. http://www.wpath.org/documents2/soc-v6.pdf (accessed 25 November 2012).

Worth, Heather (2008) 'Bad-Assed Honeys with a Difference: South Auckland *Fa'afafine* Talk about Identity', Fran Martin et al. (eds) *AsiaPacifiQueer. Rethinking Genders and Sexualities.* Urbana: University of Illinois Press, pp. 149–162.

Film Sources

'Ai to koi' (2007), *Japanorama.* [TV programme] BBC Choice, BBC Three. 26 March.

'Haruni Ai ni nani kiku?' (2010) (What will you ask Haruna Ai?), *Akashi ya tōku.* 7 September, available online at http://www.youtube.com/watch?v=_z-OKNeNP3U (accessed 1 November 2012).

Longinotto, Kim (1995 dir.). *Shinjuku Boys.*

Zajdermann, Paule (2007 dir.). *Judith Butler: Philosophical Encounters of the Third Kind.*

CONTRIBUTORS

Rebekah Clements is Research Associate at the Faculty of Asian and Middle Eastern Studies at the University of Cambridge and a Research Fellow at Queens' College, Cambridge. She completed her PhD on the history of translation in early-modern Japan in 2008, studying at the University of Cambridge (Trinity College), and is currently working on a book on the subject.

Chris Deacon graduated in 2012. During his undergraduate degree in Japanese Studies at Trinity College, Cambridge, Chris's interests and research eventually centred on modern society, in particular the field of masculinity in contemporary Japan. He is currently studying for the Graduate Diploma in Law at BPP Law School in Waterloo, and from 2014 he will train with the law firm Slaughter and May to become a solicitor.

Hattie Jones graduated from the University of Cambridge with a BA (Hons.) in Japanese Studies in 2011. She currently lives near Washington DC and is a doctoral student in Criminology and Criminal Justice at the University of Maryland. Her interests include law and crime in Japan, global security and North Korea, ethnic and linguistic minorities in criminal justice systems and intersections of crime, gender and sexuality in popular media.

Angelika Koch is a PhD candidate at the Faculty of Asian and Middle Eastern Studies at the University of Cambridge (graduating 2013). Her research interests include the history of gender, sexuality and medicine in Edo Japan. She received an MPhil in Japanese Studies and a BA in Anglophone Literatures from the University of Vienna. She also studied for six months at the Università Ca' Foscari in Venice, a year at Meiji University in Tokyo and spent six months at Ritsumeikan University on a Japan Foundation PhD Fellowship.

Nicola McDermott graduated from the University of Cambridge in 2011. After taking a year out to teach English in Tokyo, she decided to continue her line of research from her undergraduate dissertation and pursue an MA in Gender Studies at the School of Oriental and African Studies (SOAS, University of London). Her areas of interest include LGBT and queer politics in Japan but she is hoping to expand this to China by studying Mandarin.

Mark Morris is a Lecturer in East Asian Cultural History. He has written about Japanese literature and, in more recent years, the cinema of South Korea. He has supervised Japanese Studies dissertation projects on a wide range of subjects, from film and literature to social history, Japanese hiphop and jazz.

Sven Palys graduated in Japanese Studies at the University of Cambridge in 2010. After a short stint at an educational publisher in Berlin, he moved to Japan shortly after the Tohoku Earthquake of 2011 to study Japanese Media at the University of Tokyo supported by a MEXT Scholarship. His research interest focuses on identity construction in media, with particular reference to post-war Japanese music TV shows. Alongside his degree, Sven works in Japanese TV and likes to dabble in editorial design.

Brigitte Steger is Lecturer in Modern Japanese Studies at the University of Cambridge, specializing in the anthropology of daily life. Her PhD was on the social history and cultural anthropology of sleep in Japan, and she has published award-winning books and many articles on this topic. In 2011 she stayed at a tsunami evacuation shelter in Northeast Japan, where she interviewed people about their lives at the shelter. The book *Coping with Disaster* (co-edited with Tom Gill and David Slater) is scheduled to be published in spring 2013 in English (Peter Lang) and Japanese (Jinbun Shoin).

Zoya Street spent her final year at Cambridge studying religious history alongside writing the dissertation featured in this book. After graduation Zoya studied Design History at the Royal College of Art and the Victoria and Albert Museum, intending to examine early modern Japan through its material culture. A convergence of interests led to the study of Japanese videogames of the 1990s. Zoya now freelances in the games industry, working on a broad set of projects including the business site Gamesbrief as Deputy Editor, writing a crowd-funded book on the Sega Dreamcast, and dialogue writing for mobile games.

Denise Telalagic is a high school student at the International School of Prague. She is a hobby artist with a particular interest in Manga-style art, which she has been drawing for ten years. Denise is especially interested in Japanese culture. She has spent time studying the Japanese language and is hoping to live in Japan one day. Denise is interested in being involved in more art projects and can be contacted at denisetelalagic@gmail.com.

Birgit Staemmler
Chinkon kishin
Mediated Spirit Possession in Japanese New Religions

Chinkon kishin is a very little known, yet extremely important ritual of spirit possession, which was performed as a highly attractive mass ritual in Ômoto, a Japanese millenarian new religion, at the beginning of the twentieth century. This book employs anthropological and hermeneutic methodologies to unravel *chinkon kishin*'s history, illustrate its performance and analyse several key issues related to spirit possession in new religions.

BUNKA – WENHUA. Tübinger Ostasiatische Forschungen, vol. 7, 2009, 496 pp., 34,90 €, br., ISBN 3-8258-6899-0

LIT Verlag Berlin – Münster – Wien – Zürich – London
Auslieferung Deutschland / Österreich / Schweiz: siehe Impressumsseite

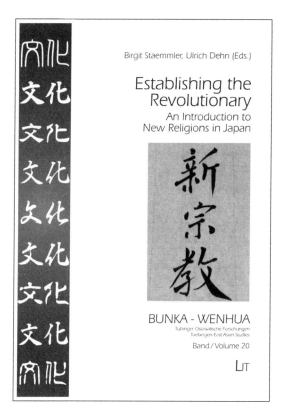

Birgit Staemmler, Ulrich Dehn (Eds.)

Establishing the Revolutionary
An Introduction to New Religions in Japan

新宗教

BUNKA - WENHUA
Tübinger Ostasiatische Forschungen
Tuebingen East Asian Studies
Band / Volume 20

LIT

Birgit Staemmler; Ulrich Dehn
Establishing the Revolutionary
An Introduction to New Religions in Japan
New Religions in Japan claim millions of members and simultaneously provoke criticism and fulfil social functions. This publication may serve as a handbook about these new religions on the basis of recent research, written by an international range of scholarly experts. The introductory chapters offer general analyses of historical, doctrinal, social, and economic aspects and hence facilitate the understanding of new religions within their overall contexts. Ten religions of major importance are introduced in detail as to their founder, circumstances of foundation, history, doctrine, present situation and activities. These are Ômoto, Seichô no Ie, Sekai Kyûseikyô, Shinnyo-en, Sôka Gakkai, Risshô Kôsei-kai, Mahikari, Kôfuku no Kagaku, Aum Shinrikyô/ Aleph/ Hikari no Wa and Chino Shôhô/ Pana-Wave Laboratory. Other important religious organisations are covered in encyclopedical references.
BUNKA – WENHUA. Tübinger Ostasiatische Forschungen, vol. 20, 2011, 408 pp., 29,90 €, br.,
ISBN-CH 978-3-643-90152-1

LIT Verlag Berlin – Münster – Wien – Zürich – London
Auslieferung Deutschland / Österreich / Schweiz: siehe Impressumsseite

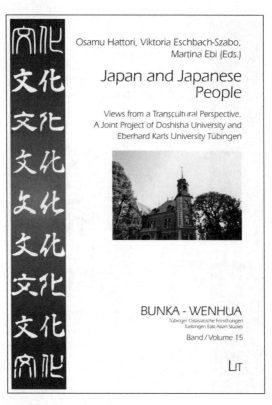

Osamu Hattori, Viktoria Eschbach-Szabo,
Martina Ebi (Eds.)

Japan and Japanese People

Views from a Transcultural Perspective.
A Joint Project of Doshisha University and
Eberhard Karls University Tübingen

BUNKA - WENHUA
Tübinger Ostasiatische Forschungen
Tuebingen East Asian Studies
Band / Volume 15

LIT

Osamu Hattori; Viktoria Eschbach-Szabo; Martina Ebi (Eds.)
Japan and Japanese People
Views from a Transcultural Perspective. A Joint Project of Doshisha University and Eberhard
Karls University Tübingen
This volume contains papers of the 2. Joint Workshop of Doshisha University and Tuebingen University
on Transcultural Studies, held in November 2009. The contributions look at Japan and Germany, at the
exchange of ideas and cultural forms, at their mutual influence and independent development in the age of
globalization from different disciplines and perspectives.
BUNKA – WENHUA. Tübinger Ostasiatische Forschungen, vol. 19, 2010, 168 pp., 34,90 €, br., ISBN 978-3-643-10616-2

LIT Verlag Berlin – Münster – Wien – Zürich – London
Auslieferung Deutschland / Österreich / Schweiz: siehe Impressumsseite

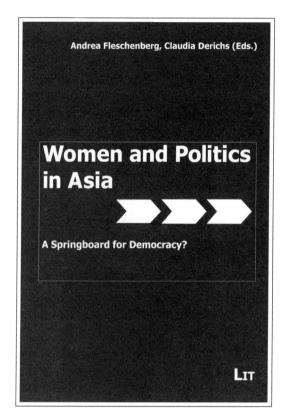

Andrea Fleschenberg; Claudia Derichs (Eds.)
Women in Politics in Asia
A Springboard for Democracy?
Why study the nexus of gender, politics and democracy in Asia? What kind of democracy and political participation can we conceptualize and identify for this heterogeneous region? In the increasingly visible Asian context, which concepts, contexts, discourses and practices do we need to reflect upon most in order to understand the complex relationship between gender and democratic processes? The authors in this book engage with precisely these crucial questions, and do so by drawing on a variety of case studies covering India, Malaysia, Indonesia and Cambodia. In the process, they scrutinize women's roles, strategies, practices and discourses on political participation and gender-inclusive political reform in various arenas of political engagement. Contributions to this volume range from studies of political actors and institutions, public policy and gender mainstreaming, political theory and citizenship discourses, to the study of various women's movements.
Politikwissenschaftliche Perspektiven, vol. 15, 2011, 184 pp., 24,90 €, br., ISBN-CH 978-3-643-90099-9

LIT Verlag Berlin – Münster – Wien – Zürich – London
Auslieferung Deutschland / Österreich / Schweiz: siehe Impressumsseite

Southeast Asian Modernities

Dagmar Hellmann-Rajanayagam, Andrea Fleschenberg
(Eds.)

Goddesses, Heroes, Sacrifices

Female Political Power in Asia

LIT

Dagmar Hellmann-Rajanayagam; Andrea Fleschenberg (Eds.)
Goddesses, Heroes, Sacrifices
Female Political Power in Asia

Women at the head of states and governments have become a regular phenomenon in South and Southeast Asia in the last decades, even though patriarchal structures have endured. A dynastic principle is seen to be at work where women are frequently preferred over available male successors. The publication discusses the relationship of the state and secularism, the significance of religion in society, the concept of the goddess, the perception and interpretation of martyrdom and sacrifice, and the question of moral capital as background for the emergence of women political leaders and their career paths.

Southeast Asian Modernities, vol. 8, 2008, 232 pp., 29,90 €, br., ISBN 978-3-8258-0540-1

LIT Verlag Berlin – Münster – Wien – Zürich – London
Auslieferung Deutschland / Österreich / Schweiz: siehe Impressumsseite

Susanne Schröter(Ed.)
Christianity in Indonesia
Perspectives of Power

Indonesia is a multicultural and multireligious nation whose heterogeneity is codified in the state doctrine, the Pancasila. Yet the relations between the various social, ethnic, and religious groups have been problematic down to the present day. In several respects, Christians have a precarious role in the struggle for shaping the nation. In the aftermath of the former president Suharto's resignation and in the course of the ensuing political changes Christians have been involved both as victims and perpetrators in violent regional clashes with Muslims that claimed thousands of lives. Since the beginning of the new millennium the violent conflicts have lessened, yet the pressure exerted on Christians by Islamic fundamentalists still continues undiminished in the Muslim-majority regions. The future of the Christians in Indonesia remains uncertain, and pluralist society is still on trial. For this reason the situation of Christians in Indonesia is an important issue that goes far beyond research on a minority, touching on general issues relating to the formation of the nation-state.

Southeast Asian Modernities, vol. 12, 2011, 424 pp., 29,90 €, gb., ISBN 978-3-643-10798-5

LIT Verlag Berlin – Münster – Wien – Zürich – London
Auslieferung Deutschland / Österreich / Schweiz: siehe Impressumsseite

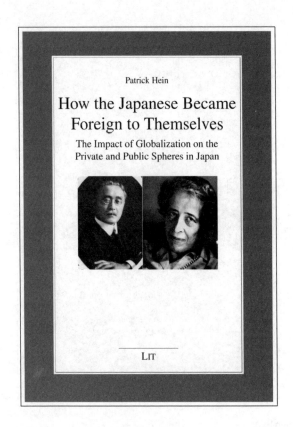

Patrick Hein

How the Japanese Became Foreign to Themselves

The Impact of Globalization on the Private and Public Spheres in Japan

The question whether Arendt's distinction of the 'private, public and society' can be applied to the Japanese cultural context will be examined. It will be argued that repressed needs for equality, plurality and independence have made their way back through increased civil political participation and that this process is driven by the renaissance of the pre Meiji Samurai principle of ethical individualism.

Politikwissenschaft, vol. 164, 2009, 240 pp., 34,90 €, br., ISBN 3-643-10085-6

LIT Verlag Berlin – Münster – Wien – Zürich – London

Auslieferung Deutschland / Österreich / Schweiz: siehe Impressumsseite